Introduction to Psychophysics with Python

Published 2026 by River Publishers
River Publishers
Broagervej 10, 9260 Gistrup, Denmark
www.riverpublishers.com

Distributed exclusively by Routledge
605 Third Avenue, New York, NY 10017, USA
4 Park Square, Milton Park, Abingdon, Oxon OX14 4RN

Introduction to Psychophysics with Python / Rakesh Sengupta and Maganti Madhavilatha.

Routledge is an imprint of the Taylor & Francis Group, an informa business

ISBN 978-87-438-0944-9 (paperback)
ISBN 978-87-438-0946-3 (online)
ISBN 978-8-743-80945-6 (ebook master)
ISBN 978-87-438-0948-7 (ePub)
DOI: 10.1201/9788743809456

Introduction to Psychophysics with Python

Rakesh Sengupta
School of Interwoven Arts and Sciences,
Krea University, India

Maganti Madhavilatha
School of Interwoven Arts and Sciences,
Krea University, India

River Publishers

Routledge
Taylor & Francis Group
NEW YORK AND LONDON

Contents

Preface

Psychophysics is at a unique intersection of psychology, neuroscience, and quantitative science – an *irreverent* approach that refuses to treat tradition as unquestionable authority and instead demands rigorous, reproducible measurement of perception. This book was written to inspire readers to challenge assumptions, embrace robust experimental design, and utilize computational tools to transform subjective experience into precise data.

Chapter 1: History of Psychophysics. We revisit the pioneering work of Weber, Fechner, and Stevens, not to idolize their methods, but to understand how early ideas were challenged, refined, and ultimately replaced by more reliable practices. Through classical paradigms, the methods of limits, constant stimuli, and adjustment, we see how the field evolved by questioning its own foundations.

Chapter 2: Understanding Sensory Systems. Armed with a critical mindset, we explore the anatomy and function of vision, audition, touch, taste, and smell. Each modality is illustrated with real-world examples and up-to-date research, highlighting where old models fell short and how modern techniques, such as color-opponent theory and binaural localization, advance our reproducible understanding.

Chapter 3: Signal Detection Theory and Experimental Design. Here we introduce the statistical and methodological toolkit that keeps psychophysics honest. From experimental designs (between and within subjects) and common pitfalls to power analysis, signal detection theory, parametric and non-parametric tests, and psychometric function fitting, this chapter offers concrete recipes for reproducible research and ways to critically evaluate your own results.

Chapter 4: Using PsychoPy to Build Experiments. In a hands-on finale, we strip away the boilerplate and guide you through building, running, and analyzing your own studies in PsychoPy. Annotated code snippets emphasize clarity, reproducibility, and version control, demonstrating how to move seamlessly from conceptual design to transparent, shareable data.

Whether you are a psychology major, neuroscience researcher, or data-curious learner, this guide empowers you to approach perception with healthy skepticism, scientific rigor, and a commitment to reproducibility.

Rakesh Sengupta *and*
Madhavilatha Maganti,
Krea University
Summer, 2025

Acknowledgements

We would like to thank our students who have taken the psychophysics course at Krea University and the teaching fellows who assisted us through the course as well as with reviewing the material for the book – especially Lekhana Priya Gundapaneni, Aniruddha Walke, Aarthi Venkatesh and Purvikalyani Prasannah. We would also like to thank the management at Krea University, the honorable Vice Chancellor Prof. Nirmala Rao and the Deans, Prof. Prithvi Datta Chandra Shobhi and Prof. Sivakumar Srinivasan for their wonderful support in setting up a research and teaching lab with ability to support behavioral and neuroimaging experiments.

Aims and Objectives

This book presents psychophysics as an *irreverent yet rigorous science* – a field that challenges past authority by emphasizing reproducibility, quantitative precision, and the empirical basis of perception. Rooted in classical traditions (Weber, Fechner, Stevens), it equips readers with both historical grounding and hands-on methods.

Overall aim: To enable undergraduate students and early-career researchers to understand, design, implement, and analyze psychophysical experiments with scientific rigor and practical competence.

Specific objectives:

- **Historical insight:** Illustrate how foundational ideas in psychophysics – Weber's JND, Fechner's logarithmic law, Stevens' power function – emerged and shaped experimental psychology.
- **Sensory foundations:** Describe the anatomy and physiology of vision, audition, touch, taste, and smell, and link these systems to concrete psychophysical paradigms (e.g. contrast sensitivity, frequency discrimination, two-point thresholds).
- **Experimental design and statistics:** Teach rigorous experimental design principles (counterbalancing, randomization, adaptive staircases), intro- duce signal detection theory and psychometric curve fitting, and provide foundations in both parametric and non-parametric analysis.
- **Hands-on PsychoPy experience:** Guide students through building complete experiments – from window setup to trial logic – in PsychoPy, including brightness JND tasks and serial memory experiments, along with real-time and post-hoc data analysis (e.g. in Google Colab).
- **Critical thinking and reproducibility:** Foster an attitude of questioning assumptions, assessing methodological limitations, and valuing clarity, transparency, and replication in empirical science.

- **Bridging theory and application:** Provide accessible examples and step-by-step tutorials so readers can translate theory into practice, whether investigating threshold detection, sensory development, or signal-to-noise discrimination.

By the end of the book, readers will be able to:

- Explain classical psychophysical laws and paradigms and critique their assumptions.
- Design and run perceptual experiments using PsychoPy.
- Analyze experimental data using descriptive statistics, signal detection metrics, and psychometric function estimation.
- Evaluate experimental designs for bias, validity, and reproducibility.
- Relate sensory physiology to perceptual measurement and everyday perceptual experiences.

For deeper coverage of statistical testing methods and psychometric modeling, readers are encouraged to consult a standard introductory statistics textbook alongside this text.

List of Abbreviations

2AFC	Two-alternative forced choice
2IFC	Two-interval forced choice
AUC	Area under the curve (ROC)
CDF	Cumulative distribution function
d′	d-prime (sensitivity in signal detection theory)
FA	False alarm rate
H	Hit rate (true positive rate)
ISI	Inter-stimulus interval
ITI	Inter-trial interval
JND	Just noticeable difference
ROC	Receiver operating characteristic (curve)
RT	Reaction time
SDT	Signal detection theory
SE	Standard error
σ	Standard deviation
VWM	Visual working memory

About the Authors

Dr. Rakesh Sengupta has been a researcher and Assistant Professor at School of Inter-woven Arts and Sciences, Krea University, Sri City, India since 2025, holding a PhD from the University of Hyderabad (2015). His interdisciplinary background spans developmental and educational psychology, cognitive and computational neuroscience, and creative cognition. With a growing scholarly record (33 publications, ~300 citations, h-index of 9) and robust collaborations across psychology and brain research communities, he brings both empirical rigor and a multicultural perspective essential for cognitive science. He is actively involved in experiments combining behavioral assessment and neuroscientific measures (e.g., EEG, eye-tracking) to explore cognitive faculties in culturally grounded settings.

Madhavilatha Maganti is an Associate Professor of Psychology at Krea University with expertise in Developmental Psychology and Cognitive Science, specializing in infancy and early childhood development. Her research examines developmental trajectories from the neonatal period to early childhood in high-risk and typically developing populations. Using behavioral and computational methods, her lab investigates mother–child interactions, perceptual and attentional processes, and language acquisition, contributing to embodied models of cognition. Additional work includes narrative-based language assessments, and studies on socio-emotional development in children.

Further, her work involves functional assessments of children with neurodevelopmental disorders using the World Health Organization's International Classification of Functioning, Disability and Health for Children and Youth (ICF-CY) framework.Taking this work further, she is involved in developing early childhood development interventions to reduce the impact of risks associated with early adversity. Her long-term objective is to leverage emerging empirical evidence from developmental science to advance translational research and promote scalable, evidence-based practices, with an emphasis on improving developmental outcomes for all children.

CHAPTER 1

History of Psychophysics

1.1 Truth and Scientific Method

Science thrives on three pillars:

- **Reliability** – Findings must hold up under repeated measurement.
- **Replicability** – Experiments should yield the same results when independently reproduced.
- **Rigor** – Methodological integrity guards against bias and error.

Science begins with observation. A single flowering plant among hundreds, or a momentary lapse of kindness in an otherwise good person, do not by themselves reveal underlying laws. However, after confirming our observation we can systematically investigate the underlying laws. In the case of the flowering plant one must go back to check why all the other instances failed (e.g., quantify soil quality, ambient light and temp, and so on). Only systematic, quantitative methods can distinguish true effects from noise.

1.2 What is Psychophysics?

Psychophysics is the branch of psychology that quantitatively investigates the relationship between physical stimuli and the sensations and perceptions they produce. It is one of the oldest and most rigorous experimental approaches in psychology, tracing its roots back to the 19th century work of Gustav, who formalized methods for relating stimulus intensities to perceived magnitudes.

DOI: 10.1201/9788743809456-1

1.2.1 Psychophysics in the scientific method

Psychophysics exemplifies the scientific method applied to human perception. It involves:

- **Observation:** Identifying phenomena such as visual brightness, loudness, or tactile pressure and how these are experienced by observers.
- **Hypothesis formation:** Proposing measurable relationships between stimulus parameters (e.g., luminance, frequency, duration) and perceptual judgments (e.g., detection, discrimination, preference).
- **Experimentation:** Using controlled environments to present stimuli and collect responses from participants.
- **Quantitative analysis:** Fitting mathematical models, such as psycho- metric functions or Weber–Fechner laws (explained in Section 1.5), to experimental data to estimate perceptual thresholds, discrimination abilities, or response biases.

This methodological cycle ensures that claims about perception are testable, replicable, and grounded in empirical data.

1.2.2 Relation to psychology

While general psychology investigates behavior and cognition broadly, psychophysics focuses specifically on the interface between the *external world* (stimulus properties) and the *internal world* (subjective experience). For instance, while a psychologist might study visual attention or memory, a psychophysicist would examine how small a difference in brightness must be for an observer to reliably detect a change.

This bridge between objective measurements and subjective experiences makes psychophysics foundational for sensory psychology, neuroscience, cognitive science, and even applied fields such as human–computer interaction and visual design.

Thus, psychophysics provides both a theoretical foundation and a methodological toolkit for understanding perception with scientific precision.

1.3 Why Psychophysics?

At its core, psychophysics asks: how do we turn a person's private sensory experience into objective data? By precisely controlling physical stimuli and recording perceptual judgments, psychophysicists uncover the rules that govern sensation. The CIELAB color space beautifully illustrates this approach [9]. Developed in 1976 by the International Commission on Illumination (CIE), CIELAB was built upon thousands of observer judgments about when two colors "look different," yielding a coordinate system in which equal geometric steps correspond to equal perceived steps in hue or chroma. In other words, what begins as a subjective "That red is more intense than that orange" becomes a reproducible measurement.

Figure 1.1 Approximate CIELAB volume: points are plotted at sampled lightness L^* levels (vertical axis) and at (a^*, b^*) coordinates (horizontal plane). Hue is encoded by the HSB hue angle, chroma by saturation, and brightness by L^*. Dashed circles indicate the maximum theoretical gamut radius at each L^*.

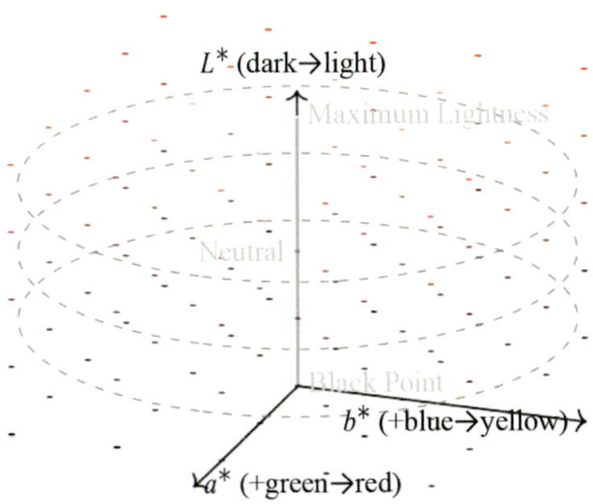

Key reasons we need psychophysics:

- *Quantification of subjectivity.* It converts personal experiences into numerical thresholds (e.g. JNDs, see Section 1.5).
- *Geometric modeling.* By mapping sensation onto spaces like CIELAB, one can visualize and predict how changes in stimulus lead to changes in perception.
- *Empirical validation.* Behavioral experiments test and refine the mathematical laws (logarithmic, power functions) that relate stimulus to sensation.

The CIELAB color space exemplifies the power of psychophysics to bridge subjective experience and quantifiable measurement. Designed in 1976 by the CIE, CIELAB's fundamental principle is that equal distances in the space correspond to approximately equal perceived color differences. This makes it an ideal framework for studying human color perception.

The dashed circles in Figure 1.1 trace out the maximum achievable chroma (color intensity) at each lightness level $L^\star$, effectively delineating the human color gamut in CIELAB. Constructing CIELAB in 1976 required extensive psychophysical scaling studies under CIE-prescribed viewing conditions, in which trained observers used the Method of Constant Stimuli and partition-scaling techniques to judge when two color patches "just began to differ" in hue or chroma. From these thousands of threshold measurements, the CIE derived non-linear transforms of the XYZ tristimulus values into $L^\star$, $a^\star$, and $b^\star$ such that equal Euclidean steps in the resulting space correspond to approximately equal perceived differences. Modern experiments build on this legacy by fitting parametric psychometric functions (e.g. cumulative Gaussians) to observer response data, allowing precise estimation of JNDs in hue, chroma, and lightness – quantifying how fine a step in stimulus is required for perception to change at a given point in the color solid (see Figure 1.2). Through CIELAB, Psychophysics demonstrates how:

Figure 1.2 A sketch of the CIELAB $a^\star b^\star$ plane (at fixed lightness $L^\star$), showing how color judgments become coordinates in a perceptual space

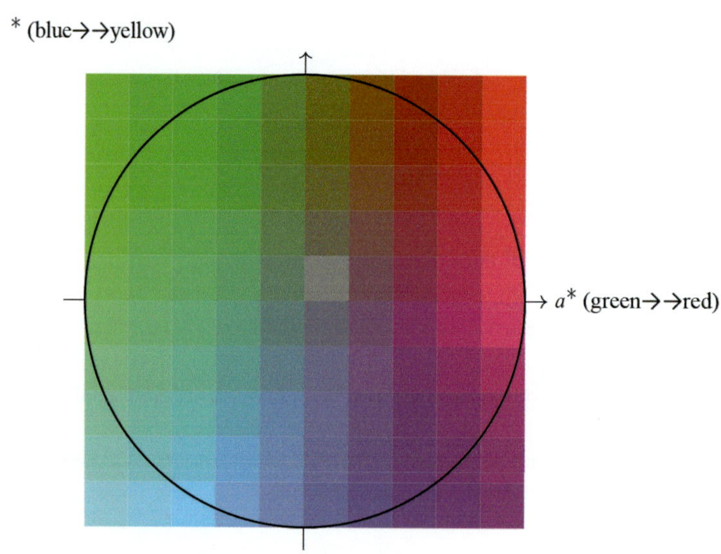

(1) Subjective experiences can be systematically measured.
(2) Perceptual phenomena can be represented geometrically.
(3) Scientific models can be validated through behavioral experiments.

This framework has practical applications in colorimetry, digital displays, and clinical vision testing – showcasing how psychophysical methods transform sensory science into technological innovation.

1.4 Timeline of Key Developments

Psychophysics has evolved through several overlapping stages, each reflecting new methods and theoretical perspectives:

(1) **Origins (1830s–1860s):** Weber's measurements of just noticeable differences (JNDs) in touch and weight [57] provided the empirical basis that formalized in 1860 as the first quantitative link between physical stimuli and sensation [11, 12].
(2) **Classical psychophysics (late 1800s–early 1900s):** Fechner's logarithmic law and the establishment of experimental laboratories (e.g., Wundt's Leipzig lab) made psychophysics the cornerstone of experimental psychology [3].
(3) **Methodological expansion (1940s–1960s):** Stevens introduced magnitude estimation and the power law [47, 48], broadening psychophysics to new sensory modalities and emphasizing direct numerical scaling of perceived intensity.
(4) **Signal detection and computerization (1970s):** Digital stimulus control and the advent of signal detection theory (SDT) allowed researchers to disentangle sensory sensitivity from decision biases, ushering in more rigorous behavioral paradigms [25].
(5) **Computational modeling and neuroimaging (2000–present):** Modern psychophysics integrates computational models of sensory coding with neuroimaging techniques, linking perceptual thresholds to neural mechanisms and cognitive theory [22, 44, 43, 54].

This historical progression mirrors psychology's shift from introspective reports to objective behavioral measures. Early psychophysics underpinned the birth of experimental psychology – mid-century advances placed it alongside other behavioral methods (reaction-time tasks, conditioning paradigms) – and today, psychophysics serves as a quantitative bridge between stimulus, behavior, and brain (Figure 1.3).

Figure 1.3 Key figures in the development of psychophysics: contributions and landmark works.

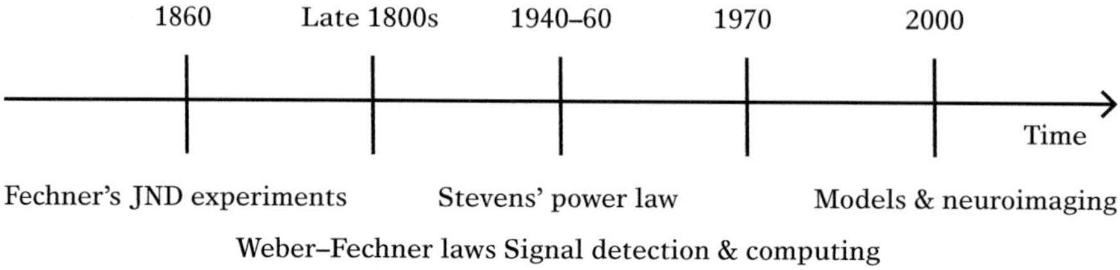

Ernst Weber (1795–1878)

Key contributions:
- First systematic measurement of the *just noticeable difference* (JND).
- Formulated the proportionality principle: $\Delta I/I = k$ (Weber's Law).

Representative works:
- *De Pulsu, Resorptione, Auditu et Tactu* (1834) [57]
- Experimental studies on weight discrimination in skin senses

Gustav Fechner (1801–1887)

Key contributions:
- Founded psychophysics as A quantitative science.
- Proposed the logarithmic relation $S = k \log I$ (Fechner's law).

Representative works:
- *Elemente der Psychophysik* (1860) [11, 12]
- Research on psychophysical measurement methods

S.S. Stevens (1906–1973)

Key contributions:
- Introduced magnitude estimation for direct scaling.
- Formulated Stevens' Power law: $S = kI^n$.

Representative works:
- *The Psychophysics of Sensory Function* (1956–1957)
- Extensive experiments across vision, hearing, and taste [47, 48]

1.5 Weber's and Fechner's Laws

Psychophysics begins with a simple but profound question: how does a change in the physical world translate into a change in perception? Two landmark principles – Weber's Law and Fechner's Law – provide the answer.

1.5.1 Weber's law

Ernst Heinrich Weber (1795–1878) was a devoted anatomist who, while lecturing on tactile sensation, noticed that people's ability to detect differences in weight depended on the weight they were already holding [57, 60]. In one classic anecdote, Weber demonstrated this by having a blindfolded subject hold a 100 g weight in one hand and a slightly heavier one in the other; the subject could reliably detect a 5 g difference, but if both weights were 1 kg, they needed about 50 g extra to notice any change. From these observations he formulated:

$$\frac{\Delta I}{I} = k,$$

where I is the base intensity, ΔI is the just-noticeable difference (JND), and k (the "Weber fraction") is roughly constant for a given sense modality (see Figure 1.4).

Figure 1.4 Visual representation of Weber's law.

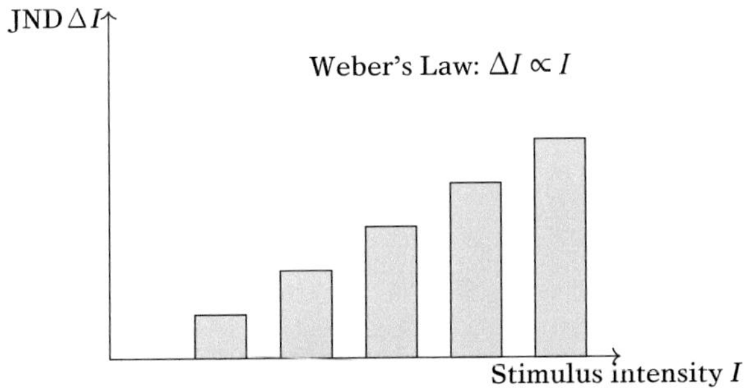

Figure 1.5 Visual representation of Fechner's law.

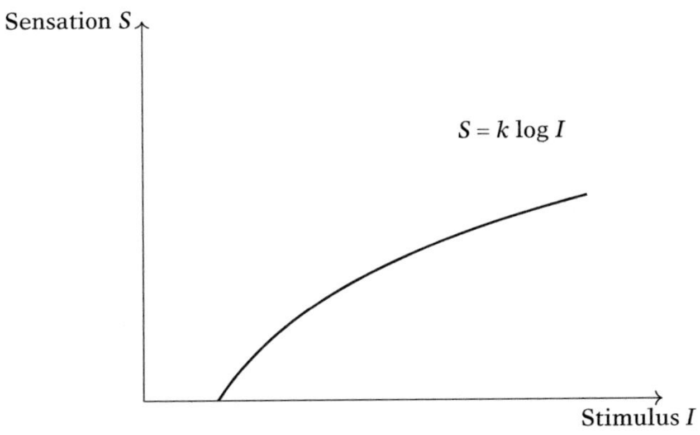

1.5.2 Fechner's Law

Gustav Theodor (1801–1887), originally trained as a physicist, turned to the mind after a bout of near-blindness forced him away from optics. In 1860 he published *Elemente der Psychophysik* [11, 12], arguing that if each JND represents an equal step in sensation, then cumulative JNDs produce a logarithmic relationship between sensation S and stimulus I:

$$S = k \log I.$$

Here, S is the perceived magnitude (in "sensory units"), I is the physical stimulus, and k is a scaling constant. Theodor's insight bridged the gap between discrete threshold data and continuous sensation (Figure 1.5) [19].

Figure 1.6 Method of limits.

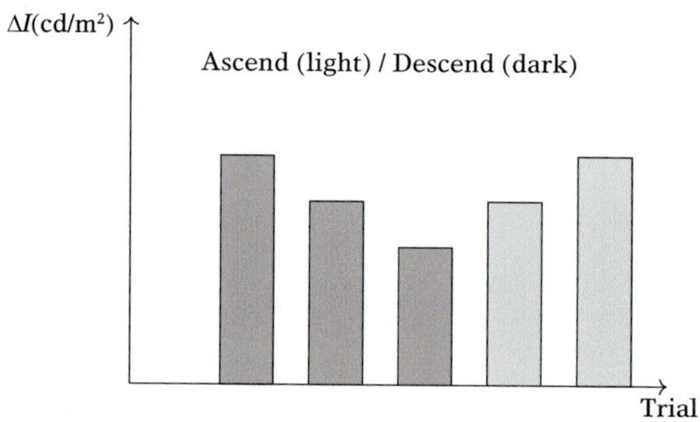

1.6 Experimental Paradigms: A Brightness JND Example

To illustrate the three classic methods in a unified context, we'll use a simple brightness discrimination task. An observer compares a reference gray patch (luminance I) to a second patch whose brightness varies by ΔI. The goal is to find the smallest ΔI that the observer can reliably detect – the just-noticeable difference (JND) [14, 3, 34, 8].

1.6.1 Method of limits

- **Procedure:** Present the comparison patch in ascending series (ΔI from small to large) until the observer first reports "brighter," then in descending series until they report "not brighter." See Figure 1.6.

- **Example:** Starting at $\Delta I = 0$, increase brightness in steps of 1 cd/m^2 until the observer says "brighter"; then decrease from 10 cd/m^2 in 1 cd/m^2 steps until "not brighter."
- **Threshold:** Average the "crossover" points from multiple ascending/descending runs.

1.6.2 Method of constant stimuli

- **Procedure:** Prepare a set of comparison brightness levels $\{\Delta I_i\}$ both below and above expected threshold. Present them in random order, asking "Is this patch brighter than the reference?"
- **Example:** Use $\Delta I = \{0, 1, 2, 3, 4, 5\}$ cd/m^2, each repeated 10 times in random sequence.
- **Threshold:** Plot proportion "brighter" vs. ΔI, read off the 75% point on the psychometric curve (Figure 1.7).

Figure 1.7 Psychometric function.

Psychometric Function

A cumulative Gaussian often models detection probability:

$$P(\Delta I) = \Phi\frac{\Delta I - \mu}{\sigma}$$

where μ is the 75% threshold (JND) and σ controls the slope (sensitivity).

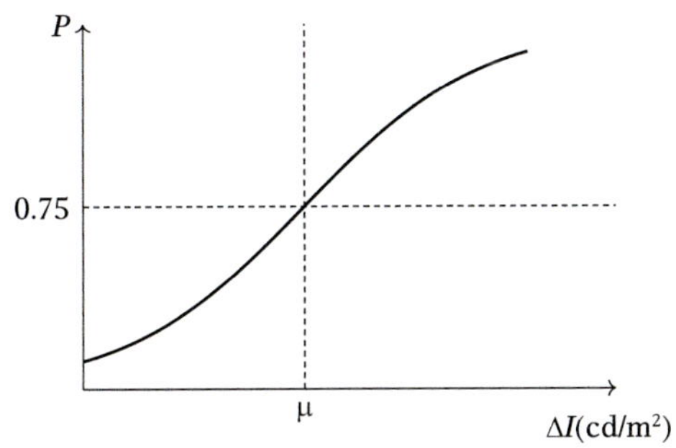

1.6.3 Method of adjustment

- **Procedure:** The observer controls a dial to adjust the comparison patch until it "just matches" the reference brightness.
- **Example:** A rotary knob varies ΔI continuously; the observer stops when the two patches appear equal.
- **Threshold:** The mean of several adjustment settings (Figure 1.8).

Figure 1.8 Threshold.

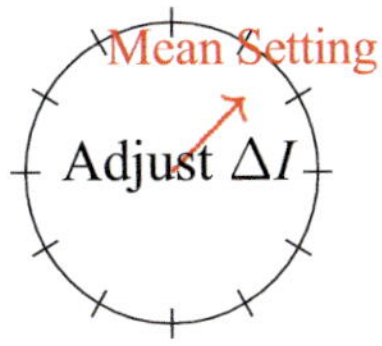

1.6.4 Comparing the methods

- **Limits** – simple, but subject to anticipation/alerting effects.
- **Constant Stimuli** – unbiased and precise but requires many trials.
- **Adjustment** – fast and intuitive, but high variability and response bias.

Modern psychophysics often combines methods (e.g. adaptive staircases within a constant-stimuli framework) and fits a parametrized psychometric function (see Figure 1.7) to obtain robust threshold estimates with fewer trials.

1.7 Preparing PsychoPy

Psychophysical experiments are now easily scripted in Python and shared reproducibly [33]. In this section, we'll walk through installation, stimulus presentation code using PsychoPy, and data analysis in Google Colab – introducing basic descriptive statistics along the way.

1.7.1 Installing PsychoPy via web resources

PsychoPy provides platform-specific installers and detailed instructions on its official website, avoiding complex dependency issues on different operating systems.

- **Windows and macOS standalone installer:** Download the latest standalone application for Windows or macOS from the PsychoPy download page, which includes all dependencies and a built-in version of Python.
- **Linux installation:** For Ubuntu and other distributions, the PsychoPy documentation recommends using either the Anaconda/Miniconda installer or building from source; see "Linux" under "Manual installations" at https://www.PsychoPy.org/download.html.
- **Conda environments:** If you manage Python environments with Conda, install PsychoPy via conda install -c conda-forge PsychoPy\index{Psychopy} as documented in the "Developers install" section of the download page.

1.8 A Simple PsychoPy Brightness JND Experiment

This experiment presents a small white dot on an otherwise dark screen. On each trial, the dot's luminance differs slightly from a fixed reference. The observer's task is a 2AFC: indicate whether the dot appears brighter or darker than the reference. Over a range of luminance offsets, we record responses and later fit a psychometric function to estimate the JND.

1.8.1 PsychoPy script

Below is the full script. Comments (#) explain each key function, especially win.flip() (which swaps the back and front buffers to display new stimuli) and core.wait() (which pauses for a fixed duration). To run your JND brightness script in PsychoPy, open the PsychoPy application and switch to the Coder view (View → Coder) where you can load your jnd brightness.py file. Once loaded, simply click the large green "Run" button in the toolbar or press F5 to execute the script directly within PsychoPy; this will launch the window, present your stimuli, and record responses as designed.

```
from PsychoPy import visual, event, core
import numpy as np
import pandas as pd

# --- Window setup ---
win = visual.Window(
    size=[800,600], # window size in pixels
    color=[0,0,0], # black background
    units='norm', # normalized: [-1,1] in both axes
    fullscr=False # set True for fullscreen
)
win.mouseVisible = False # hide cursor

# --- Stimulus parameters ---
ref_lum = 0.5 # reference luminance (0 black, 1 white)
deltas = np.linspace(-0.2, 0.2, nine := 9) # 9 steps around reference

# --- Instructions ---
instr = visual.TextStim(win,
    text="Press LEFT if the dot is darker,\nRIGHT if brighter.\n\nPress any key to begin.",
    color=[1,1,1]
)
instr.draw()
win.flip() # show instruction
event.waitKeys() # wait for any key
core.wait(0.5) # 500 ms pause before trials begin
```

```

# --- Trial loop ---
results = []
for d in deltas:
    # Create the dot with luminance = ref + delta
    dot = visual.Circle(
        win,
        radius=0.1,
        fillColor=[ref_lum + d]*3,
        lineColor=None,
        pos=(0,0)
    )
    dot.draw() # draw on back buffer
    win.flip() # display the dot
    # Keep it on screen for 500 ms
    core.wait(0.5)

    # Collect a response
    keys = event.waitKeys(
        keyList=[‘left’,‘right’,‘escape’]
    )
    if ‘escape’ in keys:
        break
    response = ‘brighter’ if keys[0]==‘right’ else ‘darker’

    # Log the offset and the response
    results.append({‘delta’: d, ’response’: response})

    # Clear the screen for 250 ms before next trial
    win.flip()
    core.wait(0.25)

# --- Save data ---
df = pd.DataFrame(results)
df.to_csv(’jnd_brightness_data.csv’, index=False)

# --- Cleanup ---
win.close()
core.quit()
```

1.8.2 Analysis in Google Colab: Step by step explanation

Once you have downloaded jnd brightness data.csv, open a new Colab notebook and follow these annotated steps. We'll explain what each library does and why we use it.

(1) **Import libraries and load data**

We begin by importing the key Python packages:

- pandas (pd): for data loading and table-based manipulation.
- numpy (np): for numerical operations (arrays, interpolation).
- matplotlib.pyplot (plt): for plotting graphs.
- scipy.optimize.curve fit: to fit our psychometric model to data.
- scipy.stats.norm: for the cumulative Gaussian (normal CDF).

Listing 1.1 Step 1: Import and load

```
import pandas as pd # table handling
import numpy as np # arrays & math
import matplotlib.pyplot as plt # plotting
from scipy.optimize import curve_fit # model fitting
from scipy.stats import norm # normal CDF

# Load the recorded responses into a DataFrame
df = pd.read_csv('jnd_brightness_data.csv')
df.head() # preview first five rows
```

(2) **Convert responses to numeric and summarize**

We map the categorical responses ("brighter"/"darker") to binary values (1/0). Then we group by luminance offset ΔL and compute: count = number of trials at each offset, prop = proportion judged "brighter," sd = standard deviation of the binary responses.

```
# 1 = brighter, 0 = darker
df['resp_bin'] = (df['response']=='brighter').astype(int)

# Group by offset and compute descriptive stats
grouped = df.groupby('delta').resp_bin.agg(
    count='count',
    prop='mean', # mean of 0/1 gives proportion
    sd='std' # variability at each delta
).reset_index()
grouped
```

(3) **Visualize data with error bars**

We plot ΔL on the x-axis and the proportion "brighter" on the y-axis, with error bars showing ±1 standard deviation.

Listing 1.2 Step 3: Plot with error bars

```
plt.errorbar(
    grouped['delta'],
    grouped['prop'],
    yerr=grouped['sd'],
    fmt='o-', # circles connected by lines
    capsize=5 # length of error bar caps
)
plt.axhline(0.5, color='gray', linestyle='--') # chance level
plt.xlabel('Luminance Offset deltaL')
plt.ylabel('P("Brighter")')
plt.title('Psychometric Data: Proportion Brighter')
plt.grid(True)
plt.show()
```

(4) **Define and fit the cumulative Gaussian**

A cumulative Gaussian function $P(\Delta L) = \Phi\ (\Delta L\ \mu)/\sigma$ captures the S-shaped psychometric curve. μ is the threshold (JND) at 50

Listing 1.3 Step 4: Fit psychometric function

```
# Psychometric model: cumulative normal
def cum_gauss(x, mu, sigma):
    return norm.cdf((x - mu) / sigma)

# Initial guesses: mu=0, sigma=0.1
popt, pcov = curve_fit(
    cum_gauss,
    grouped['delta'],
    grouped['prop'],
    p0=[0, 0.1]
)
mu, sigma = popt
print(f"Estimated JND (mu): {mu:.3f}")
print(f"Slope (sigma): {sigma:.3f}")
```

(5) **Overlay fit on data**

Finally, we generate a smooth curve from the fitted parameters and overlay it on the empirical data to visualize model agreement.

Listing 1.4 Step 5: Plot fit

```
# Generate fine-grained offsets
x_fine = np.linspace(grouped['delta'].min(),
                     grouped['delta'].max(), 200)
y_fit = cum_gauss(x_fine, mu, sigma)

plt.plot(x_fine, y_fit, '-', label='Cumulative Gaussian fit')
plt.scatter(grouped['delta'], grouped['prop'], color='black',
            label='Data')
plt.axvline(mu, color='gray', linestyle='--',
            label=f'JND ~ {mu:.3f}')
plt.xlabel('deltaL')
plt.ylabel('P("Brighter")')
plt.title('Psychometric Function Fit')
plt.legend()
plt.grid(True)
plt.show()
```

What's happening under the hood?

- pandas.read csv: reads the CSV into a structured DataFrame.
- numpy.linspace: generates evenly spaced luminance offsets in the PsychoPy script (reverse usage here for plotting).
- matplotlib.errorbar/plot: handles data visualization and styling.
- scipy.optimize.curve fit: finds the best-fitting parameters (μ, σ) by minimizing squared error between model and data.
- scipy.stats.norm.cdf: computes the cumulative normal distribution for each offset.

1.9 Conclusion

In this chapter, we traced the origins and evolution of psychophysics – from Weber's pioneering measurements of just-noticeable differences to Fechner's formulation of a logarithmic law of sensation. We explored classical experimental paradigms (limits, constant stimuli, adjustment) and saw how modern implementations in PsychoPy – combined with Python-based analysis in Google Colab – allow us to collect, visualize, and model psychometric data with reproducible precision.

Key takeaways:

- *Quantitative foundations:* Weber's law ($\Delta I/I = k$) and Fechner's law ($S = k \log I$) transformed subjective reports into mathematical relationships.
- *Experimental rigor:* The method of limits, constant stimuli, and adjustment remain central to measuring sensory thresholds, now enhanced by adaptive staircases and signal detection frameworks.
- *Computational tools:* PsychoPy scripts automate stimulus presentation, while Python libraries (Pandas, Matplotlib, SciPy) enable comprehensive data analysis – from descriptive statistics to psychometric function fitting.

Looking forward, psychophysics continues to expand:

- *Adaptive methods:* Bayesian staircases (e.g. QUEST+, Psi) offer faster, more efficient threshold estimates.
- *Multisensory integration:* New paradigms probe how cues from different senses combine perceptually.
- *Neuro-computational links:* Integrating psychophysical thresholds with neural recordings and computational models bridges behavior, brain, and algorithmic theory.

By uniting rigorous experimental design, open-source software, and robust statistical modeling, modern psychophysics stands at the forefront of sensory science – continuing Fechner's legacy by quantifying how we perceive the world.

1.10 Exercises: History of Psychophysics

Below are a few thought-provoking exercises to deepen your understanding of the historical development of psychophysics and the motivations behind classical paradigms.

(1) **Reconstructing Weber's experiment.** Ernst Weber measured just-noticeable differences (JNDs) for weight discrimination using metal weights.
   - Describe how you would set up a simple replication of Weber's method of limits for weight discrimination using modern laboratory tools (e.g., digital force sensors).
   - Identify potential confounding factors Weber might not have controlled for (e.g., temperature, participant posture) and propose how to address them.

(2) **Fechner's logarithmic law in context.** Gustav Fechner proposed $S = k \log I$.

- Explain the philosophical and experimental rationale behind introducing a logarithmic relation between sensation and stimulus intensity.
- Consider modern examples (e.g., perceived loudness or brightness). How does the logarithmic function reflect everyday sensory experience?

(3) **Stevens' power law and its critique.** S. S. Stevens suggested $S = kI^n$.

- Compare and contrast Stevens' proposal with Fechner's law. Under what experimental conditions might a power function fit data better than a logarithm?
- Design a brief thought experiment (e.g., brightness matching or loudness scaling) that could reveal a power-law relationship and explain how you would analyze the data.

(4) **Evaluating classical paradigms.** The method of limits, constant stimuli, and adjustment were introduced in the 19th century.

- For each method, list one strength and one limitation in the historical context (e.g., time-consuming, observer bias).
- Propose a way to modernize each paradigm using adaptive staircases or computerized control and discuss how this change improves reliability and efficiency.

(5) **Historical reflection.** Early psychophysics emerged in an era when psychology was not yet an experimental science.

- Reflect on how the emphasis on quantitative measurement in psychophysics influenced the development of experimental psychology and cognitive science.
- Consider the term "irreverent psychology" (questioning authority). Identify one historical debate or critique (e.g., challenges to introspection) and discuss how that shaped the evolution of psychophysical methods.

1.11 Further Reading

For those interested in delving deeper into the origins and evolution of Psychophysics, the following two references provide foundational context and commentary:

- Fechner, G. T. (1860/1966). *Elemente der Psychophysik.* Translated and edited by H. Adler as *Elements of Psychophysics.*
- Stevens, S. S. (1957). "On the psychophysical law." *Psychological Review*, 64(3), 153–181.

CHAPTER

2

Understanding Sensory Systems

2.1 Introduction

Sensory systems are integral to how organisms perceive and interact with their environment. They detect various forms of stimuli – light, sound, chemical compounds, and mechanical pressure – and convert them into neural signals through a process known as **transduction**. These signals are then interpreted by the brain, resulting in perception.

Definition 1: Sensory modality. A **sensory modality** refers to a specific system that responds to a particular type of stimulus. The five primary sensory modalities are:

- **Vision** – detection of light.
- **Audition** – detection of sound.
- **Touch (somatosensation)** – detection of pressure, temperature, and pain.
- **Taste (gustation)** – detection of chemical substances in food.
- **Smell (olfaction)** – detection of airborne chemical substances.

2.1.1 Sensory modalities and their functions

Each sensory modality has specialized receptors and neural pathways:

- **Vision:** Photoreceptors in the retina (rods and cones) detect light and color, transmitting signals to the visual cortex for image processing.

DOI: 10.1201/9788743809456-2

- **Audition:** Hair cells in the cochlea respond to sound vibrations, sending auditory information to the auditory cortex.
- **Touch (somatosensation):** Mechanoreceptors, thermoreceptors, and nociceptors in the skin and tissues detect pressure, temperature, and pain, relaying information to the somatosensory cortex.
- **Taste (gustation):** Taste buds on the tongue contain chemoreceptors that identify sweet, sour, salty, bitter, and umami flavors, communicating with the gustatory cortex.
- **Smell (olfaction):** Olfactory receptors in the nasal cavity detect odor molecules, sending signals directly to the olfactory bulb and cortex.

Understanding these sensory modalities provides a foundation for exploring how organisms interpret their environment. Each system's unique receptors and neural pathways contribute to the rich tapestry of perception. Subsequent sections will delve deeper into the anatomy, physiology, and processing mechanisms of each sensory modality.

Historical Perspective

Evolution of Sensory Understanding:

- **Aristotle (4th century BCE):** In *De Anima*, Aristotle proposed five canonical senses but considered touch problematic, noting: *"It is a problem whether touch is a single sense or a group of senses."* [4]
- **Galileo Galilei (1623):** In *The Assayer*, Galileo argued that vision's "action-at-a-distance" properties made it fundamentally different from contact-based mechanical senses, emphasizing the mathematical nature of sensory experiences [36].
- **Johannes Peter Müller (1835):** Introduced the *Doctrine of Specific Nerve Energies*, asserting that the nature of perception is defined by the pathway over which sensory information is carried, not by the stimulus itself [37].

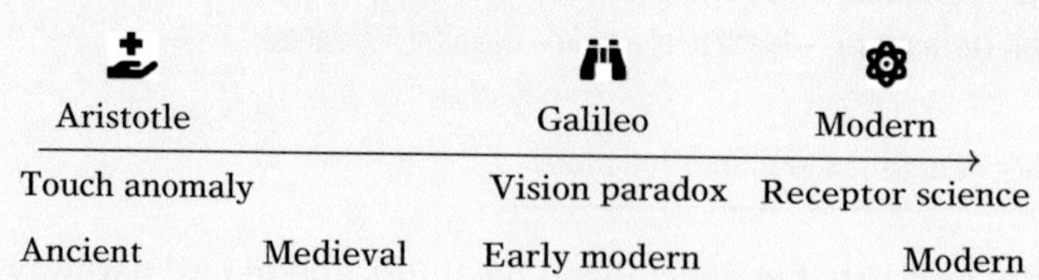

2.2 Sensation vs. Perception

Definition 2: Sensation. The process by which sensory receptors and nervous systems receive and represent stimulus energies from the environment (Figure 2.1). Biological process involving:

- Physical stimulus detection
- Receptor activation
- Neural signal transmission.

Definition 3: Perception. The process of organizing and interpreting sensory information, enabling meaningful understanding. Psychological process involving:

- Sensory integration
- Pattern recognition
- Cognitive interpretation.

Figure 2.1 From sensation to perception: Information processing pathway [29].

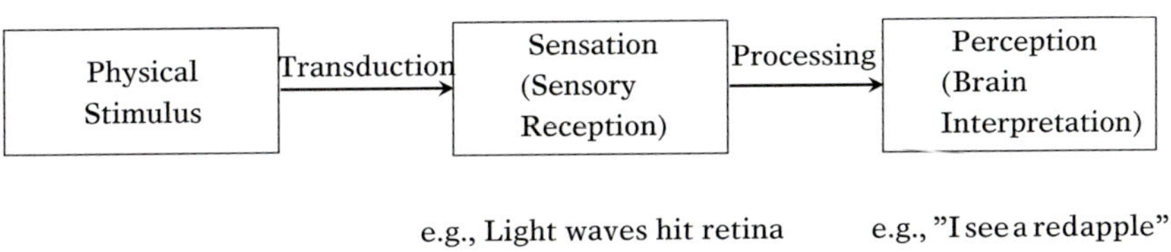

Key differences

Sensation	Perception
Raw data input	Interpreted information
Bottom-up processing	Top-down processing
Universal biological process	Subjective experience
Measured physiologically	Studied behaviorally

Examples

Example 1: McGurk effect. When the auditory sensation of "ba" combines with the visual sensation of "ga" lip movements, perception results in hearing "da" – this demonstrates sensory integration in perception [51].

Example 2: Phantom limb. Amputees may perceive sensations from missing limbs – this shows perception can occur without corresponding sensation [31].

2.2.1 Clinical relevance

- **Visual agnosia:** Normal sensation but impaired perception (can't recognize objects).
- **Diabetic neuropathy:** Impaired sensation with normal perception (can't feel feet but understands position).
- **Synesthesia**: Cross-sensory perception (hearing colors, tasting words).

Figure 2.2 Perception as interaction between sensation (bottom-up) and cognition (top-down) [45].

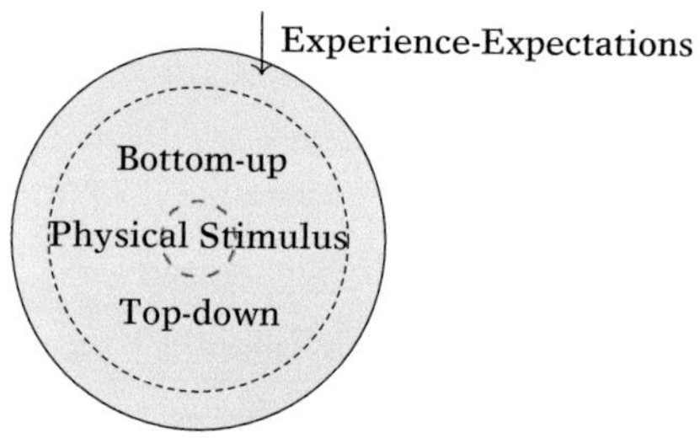

Example 3: Text perception. Try reading "Th quck brown fox jumps ovr the lzy dog". Despite altered characters (sensation), perception reconstructs meaningful text through top-down processing (Figure 2.2).

2.3 Vision

Vision is the process by which light is captured by the eye and transformed into neural signals.

2.3.1 Anatomy and optics of the eye

The eye functions like a camera, focusing light onto the retina (See Figure 2.3) [1]:

- **Cornea and lens:** refract and focus light.
- **Iris and pupil:** regulate light entry.
- **Retina:** multi-layered photoreceptive tissue.
- **Optic nerve:** carries signals to the brain.

Photoreceptors are the specialized neurons in the retina that absorb photons and initiate vision. There are two main types:

- **Rods:** extremely light-sensitive, mediate scotopic (low-light) vision, but do not distinguish color.
- **Cones:** less sensitive, mediate photopic (daylight) and color vision; three subtypes (L, M, S) tuned to long, medium, and short wavelengths.

Figure 2.3 Schematic diagrams of the human eye. Left, front (anterior) view showing pupil, iris, lens and retina. Right, sagittal (side) view showing cornea, lens, retina and optic nerve.

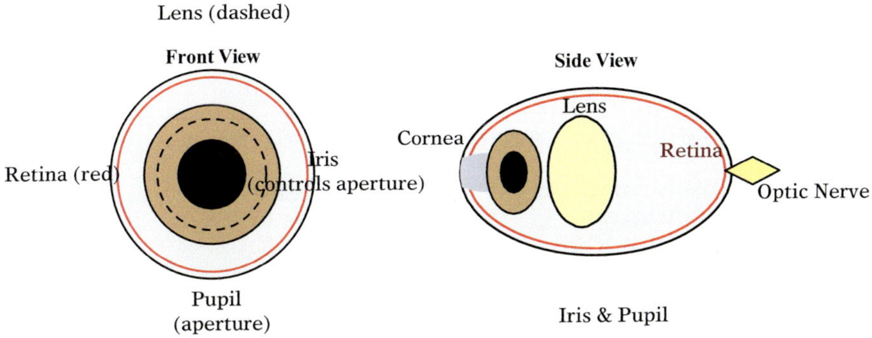

Opsin origins

Early photoreceptors evolved from light-sensitive proteins called *opsins*, which are found across all animal phyla. These G-protein-coupled receptors likely originated more than 600 million years ago in simple marine organisms, enabling basic light detection and circadian regulation.

Vertebrate duplication

In vertebrates, an ancient gene duplication gave rise to multiple opsin classes. This diversification produced the three cone subtypes (L/M/S), underpinning trichromatic color vision in primates and other mammals.

Together, rods and cones convert different ranges of light intensity and wavelength into electrical signals, setting the stage for complex processing in downstream retinal circuits and visual pathways.

Once photons are captured by rods and cones, the retina begins to encode color and contrast using *center–surround receptive fields* (Figure 2.4) and *opponent channels* (Figure 2.5). Rather than emphasizing the detailed biochemistry, we focus here on how cones feed into "on–off" channels and color-opponent pathways.

Definition 4: Center–surround receptive field. A **center–surround** receptive field has a small central region ("center") where light increases (or decreases) the ganglion cell's firing rate, and a surrounding annulus ("surround") where the opposite occurs [7]. This arrangement enhances contrast at edges.

Figure 2.4 Schematic receptive fields of ON–center and OFF–center retinal ganglion cells.

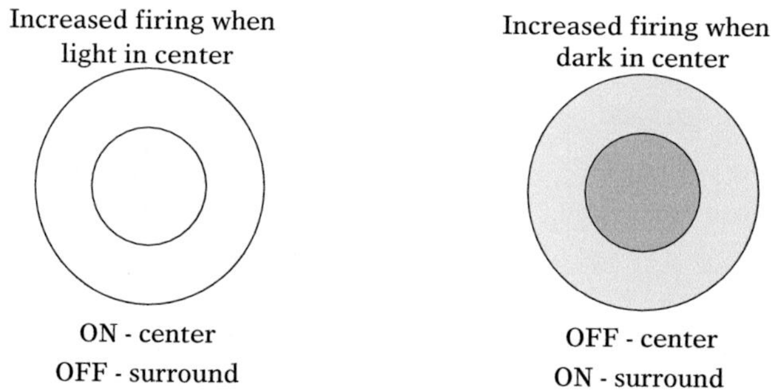

Edge detection. An ON–center cell responds strongly to a bright bar on a dark background, highlighting *light–dark* edges.

Spot detection. An OFF–center cell signals the appearance of a dark spot on a bright surface, useful for detecting shadows and textures.

Photoreceptor signals (L, M, S cones) are recombined in the retina and lateral geniculate nucleus (LGN) into opponent channels [15]:

Red–green channel: $(L - M)$

Blue–yellow channel: $\left(S - \frac{L+M}{2}\right)$

Luminance channel: $(L + M)$.

Consider a striped flag with red and green bars. The red–green channel signals *differences* between adjacent stripes, making the boundary sharply visible even under low contrast.

These opponent and on–off mechanisms form the foundation for all higher- order visual processing – enhancing edges, contrasts, and colors before information reaches primary visual cortex (V1).

Figure 2.5 Simplified diagram of color-opponent processing in the LGN. Red–green and blue– yellow channels compute differences between cone signals, while the luminance channel sums L and M cone signals. These opponent channels enhance color contrast and form the basis for subsequent color processing in the visual cortex.

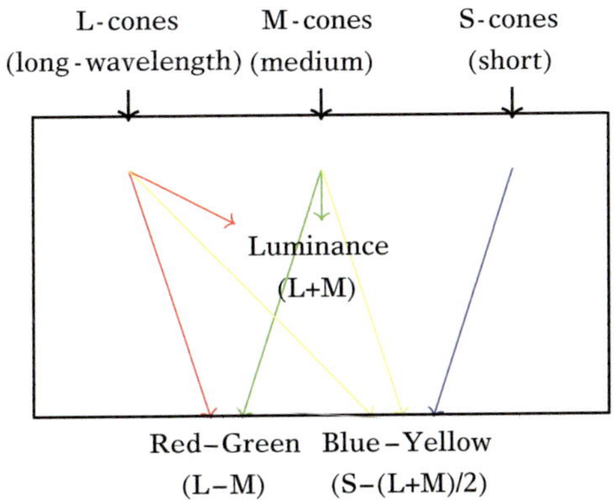

2.3.2 Dual visual pathways

After leaving the retina, signals travel via the optic nerve and chiasm to the lateral geniculate nucleus (LGN) of the thalamus, and from there into primary visual cortex (V1). From V1, information is routed along two major cortical streams (Figure 2.6):

- **Ventral stream** ("what" pathway):
  LGN → V1 → V2 → V4 → inferotemporal cortex (IT/FFA).
  Specialized for object and face recognition, color processing, and detailed form analysis.
- **Dorsal stream** ("where/how" pathway):
  LGN → V1 → V2 → MT/V5 → posterior parietal cortex (PPC/LIP).
  Specialized for motion detection, spatial localization, and visually guided actions such as reaching and eye movements.

Fusiform face area (FFA)

The FFA in ventral temporal cortex responds selectively to faces. Lesions here can cause prosopagnosia (face blindness) despite intact object recognition.

Figure 2.6 Major cortical and subcortical pathways: the ventral "what" stream (yellow) for object/face recognition (including FFA), the dorsal "where/how" stream (orange) for motion and action (including LIP), and the superior colliculus (green) mediating reflexive eye movements [21].

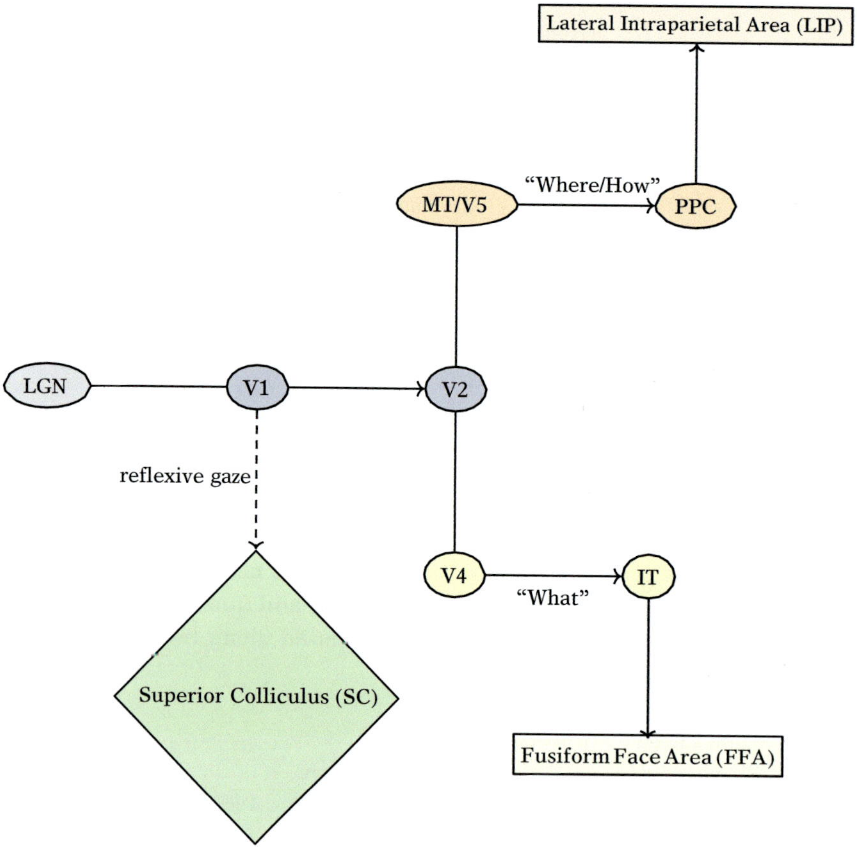

Lateral intraparietal area (LIP)

LIP neurons encode spatial attention and saccade planning. Activity here reflects where the eyes will move next, integrating motion and salience signals.

Superior colliculus (SC)

The SC in the midbrain receives direct retinal input and guides rapid, reflexive eye movements (saccades), essential for orienting to novel stimuli.

For instance, when tracking a moving ball, the dorsal stream (MT → PPC → LIP) calculates the ball's velocity and guides smooth pursuit, while sudden peripheral flashes activate SC circuits to trigger rapid saccades for foveating the target [16].

2.3.3 Visual psychophysics paradigms

Psychophysics provides controlled methods for probing the limits and mechanisms of human vision. Here we describe four core paradigms, their purposes, typical protocols, and illustrative examples.

Contrast sensitivity function (CSF)

Purpose: Determining the smallest contrast at which sinusoidal gratings of different spatial frequencies can be detected. The CSF reveals the visual system's tuning to fine versus coarse detail [5].

Protocol example:

(1) Present a grating stimulus (e.g. vertical bars) at a fixed spatial frequency f and initial high contrast.
(2) Use a staircase (method of limits) to decrease contrast in steps until the observer can no longer reliably detect the grating.

(3) Repeat for multiple frequencies (e.g. 0.5, 1, 2, 4, 8 cycles/degree).
(4) Plot sensitivity $S(f) = 1/C_{\text{threshold}}(f)$ versus f.

Definition 5: Contrast sensitivity. The **contrast sensitivity** $S(f)$ at spatial frequency f is

$$S(f) = \frac{1}{C_{\text{threshold}}(f)},$$

where $C_{\text{threshold}}$ is the minimum Michelson contrast needed for detection.

Gabor patch stimulus

Gabor patches – sinusoidal gratings multiplied by a Gaussian envelope – are the gold standard stimuli in visual psychophysics. They combine a well-defined spatial frequency (cycles per degree) with precise localization. Because their Fourier transform is also Gaussian-shaped, they allow researchers to probe the tuning of neurons and perceptual channels in both the spatial and frequency domains. Typical uses include:

- **Contrast sensitivity:** Measuring thresholds at different spatial frequencies with minimal edge artifacts.
- **Orientation tuning:** Determining the angular selectivity of cortical neurons by varying patch orientation.
- **Spatial attention:** Examining how attention modulates sensitivity to localized features.

Figure 2.7 2D Gabor-like patch: three horizontal sinusoidal cycles (across four units) masked by a circular aperture, brightness modulated from black to white.

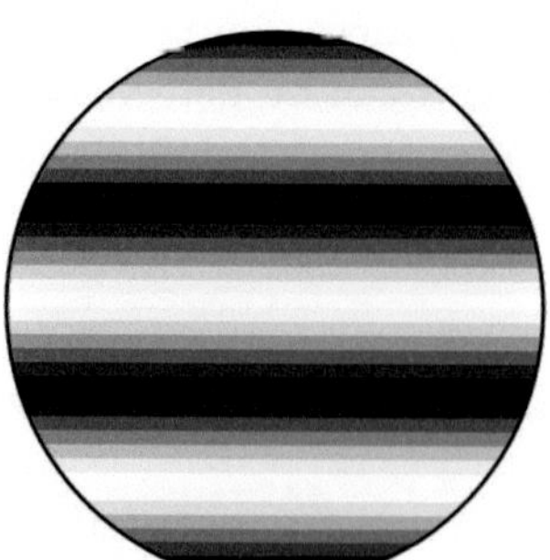

Temporal and spatial masking

Purpose: Assess how the visibility of a target stimulus is reduced (masked) by a preceding (forward masking), simultaneous (simultaneous masking), or following (backward masking) stimulus, or by surrounding patterns [32].

Protocol example:

(1) Display a brief target (e.g. a Gabor patch, see Figure 2.7) for 50 ms.
(2) Present a mask – either a high-contrast noise patch at the same location (spatial) or a second grating before/after the target (temporal).
(3) Use a 2AFC task: target appears in one of two intervals; the observer indicates which interval contained the target.
(4) Vary mask intensity or timing (stimulus onset asynchrony) to quantify Masking strength.

Adaptation experiments

Purpose: Probe neural selectivity by measuring aftereffects following prolonged exposure to a stimulus, revealing adaptation in specific channels (e.g. motion, orientation, contrast) [52].

Protocol example:

(1) Adapt observer to a high-contrast grating drifting rightward for 30 s.
(2) Present a stationary test grating and ask observer to judge perceived motion direction.
(3) The *motion aftereffect* (MAE) induces illusory motion opposite the adapting direction, demonstrating direction-selective adaptation in cortical neurons.

Example: Tilt aftereffect

Adapting to a tilted grating (e.g. +15° from vertical) for 20 s causes a subsequent vertical grating to appear tilted in the opposite direction (–15°). This reveals orientation-selective channels in V1.

Two-alternative forced-choice (2AFC)

Purpose: Minimize criterion and guessing biases by having the observer choose between two intervals or locations, one containing the stimulus and one blank or containing a reference [2].

Protocol example (Figure 2.8):

(1) Each trial consists of two intervals separated by a tone.
(2) A faint target appears in one interval; the other contains only background.
(3) Observer presses "1" or "2" to indicate which interval contained the target.
(4) Staircase procedure adjusts target intensity to converge on 75% correct.

Figure 2.8 Schematic of a 2AFC trial: two time intervals separated by a tone; the observer indicates which contained the target stimulus.

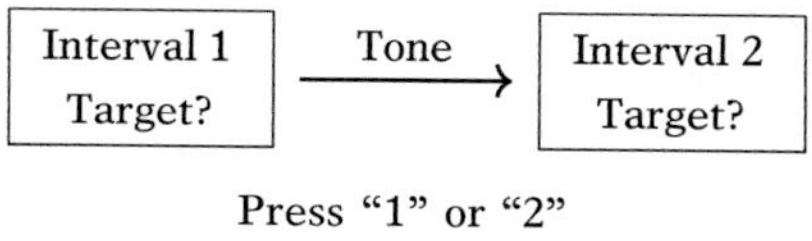

By combining these paradigms – CSF for spatial tuning, masking for contextual interactions, adaptation for channel selectivity, and 2AFC for bias-free thresholds – visual psychophysics provides a powerful toolkit for elucidating the rules governing perception.

Understanding eye optics, phototransduction, dual cortical streams, and psychophysical methods lays the groundwork for exploring higher-order visual functions such as depth perception, object recognition, and visual attention in subsequent chapters.

2.4 Audition

Audition is the process by which pressure fluctuations in air (sound waves) are converted into neural signals that the brain interprets as pitch, loudness, timbre, and spatial location.

2.4.1 Anatomy of the ear

The auditory system is responsible for our sense of hearing. It works by converting sound waves into electrical signals that the brain can interpret. This process involves three main parts of the ear: the outer ear, which collects sound waves; the middle ear, which amplifies these vibrations; and the inner ear, where the vibrations are transduced into neural signals that travel along the auditory nerve to the brain (Figure 2.9) [38].

Figure 2.9 Simple schematic of the human ear: outer ear (pinna and ear canal) collects and funnels sound; middle ear (tympanic membrane and ossicles) converts air pressure to mechanical motion; inner ear (cochlea) transduces mechanical waves into neural impulses transmitted by the auditory nerve.

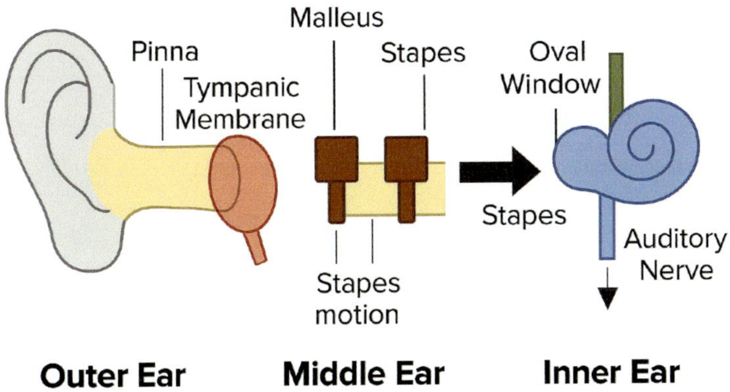

The cochlea in the inner ear transforms incoming sound waves into neural signals via two complementary encoding schemes [23, 41].

- **Place coding (tonotopy):** The basilar membrane is a tapered, elastic structure whose stiffness decreases from base to apex (Figure 2.10). High-frequency sounds cause maximal vibration near the stiff base, while low-frequency sounds peak near the flexible apex. Auditory nerve fibers synapse at specific locations, creating a spatial map of frequency along the cochlear spiral.
- **Rate coding (loudness):** Inner hair cells transduce mechanical vibrations into neurotransmitter release. As sound intensity (decibels SPL) increases, auditory nerve fiber firing rates rise and more fibers become active, encoding loudness through both the spike rate of individual fibers and the number of recruited fibers.

Inferior colliculus and beyond

After the cochlear nucleus and superior olive, signals converge in the *inferior colliculus* (midbrain) and then ascend to the *medial geniculate nucleus* (thalamus) before reaching the primary auditory cortex (A1) in the temporal lobe.

Figure 2.10 Tonotopic mapping on the basilar membrane: high frequencies (e.g., 16 kHz) activate regions near the base, while low frequencies (e.g., 200 Hz) activate regions near the apex. The basilar membrane's mechanical properties create a place code for frequency, with different regions resonating preferentially to different frequencies. This spatial representation of frequency is preserved in neural signals transmitted via the auditory nerve [40].

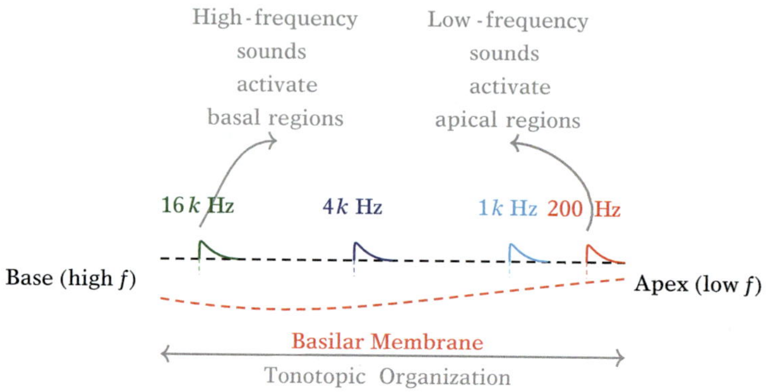

Auditory nerve fiber types

Auditory nerve fibers are classified by their spontaneous firing rates and thresholds:

- **High-SR fibers:** High spontaneous rate, low threshold – sensitive to soft sounds.
- **Low-SR fibers:** Low spontaneous rate, high threshold – extend dynamic range for loud sounds.

Together, these fiber populations encode intensity across a broad range (0–120 dB SPL).

Loudness growth

Loudness perception follows a compressive function:

$$R(I) \propto (I - I_0)^{\alpha}, \qquad 0 < \alpha < 1,$$

where R is the average firing rate, I is the sound intensity, I_0 is thethreshold intensity, and $\alpha \approx 0.3$ for human hearing.

Example 4: Frequency discrimination. At 1 kHz, the just-noticeable frequency difference ($\Delta f/f$) is approximately 0.2%, meaning you can distinguish a 2 Hz change around 1000 Hz. This precision arises from the sharp tuning of basilar membrane vibrations and corresponding auditory nerve fiber tuning curves.

2.4.2 Sound localization cues

Localization of sound sources in the horizontal and vertical planes relies on several complementary cues [30]:

- **Interaural time difference (ITD).** The difference in arrival time of a sound at the two ears. For a source directly to one side, the path to the far ear is longer by roughly the head diameter ($\approx$20 cm), creating a maximum ITD of ~600μs. ITDs are most effective for low-frequency sounds (<1.5 kHz) whose wavelengths exceed head size.
- **Interaural level difference (ILD).** The difference in sound pressure level between ears due to head shadowing. High-frequency sounds (>1.5 kHz) are attenuated by the head, producing ILDs up to 20 dB and aiding localization of high-pitched tones.
- **Spectral (monaural) cues.** Reflections and diffractions by the pinna introduce frequency-dependent notches in the sound spectrum that vary with elevation. These spectral patterns, learned through experience, allow vertical and front–back discrimination.

Definition 6: Interaural time difference.

$$\mathrm{ITD} = \frac{d_{far} - d_{near}}{c},$$

where d_{far} and d_{near} are the path lengths to the far and near ear, and c is the speed of sound.

Example: Low-frequency ITD

When a 500 Hz tone is played to your right, auditory neurons in the medial superior olive detect the microsecond delay to the left ear, signaling the source is on the right (Figure 2.11).

Figure 2.11 Interaural cues: a sound source on the left creates a time delay (Δt) to the right ear and a level difference (ΔL) due to head shadowing.

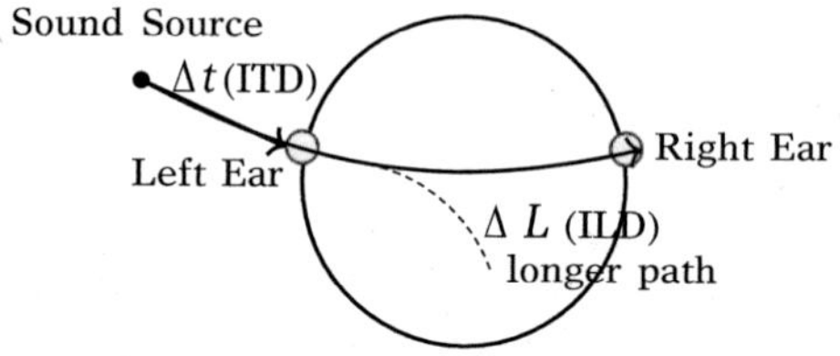

Spectral cue example

A vertical sound source (e.g. a bird overhead) produces a characteristic notch at 8 kHz in the pinna-filtered spectrum. Listeners learn to associate this notch with elevation.

2.4.3 Auditory psychophysics paradigms

Auditory psychophysics employs controlled behavioral methods to map how we detect and discriminate sounds [20]. Here we describe four foundational paradigms, their goals, typical protocols, and illustrative examples.

Pure-tone audiometry

Goal: Measure the softest tone detectable at standard audiometric frequencies (125 Hz–8 kHz).

Protocol:

(1) Present pure-tone bursts in one ear via headphones.
(2) Use a *method of limits* or 2AFC staircase: decrease level until "no tone," increase until "tone heard."
(3) Threshold is the average level at which detection switches.
(4) Plot threshold (dB SPL or dB HL) versus frequency → *audiogram.*

Frequency discrimination

Goal: Find the smallest detectable change Δf at a base frequency f.

Protocol:

(1) Adaptive 2AFC: two sequential tones, one at f and one at $f+\Delta f$.
(2) Observer indicates which was higher in pitch.
(3) Staircase adjusts Δf to converge on 75
(4) Report Weber fraction $\Delta f/f$.

Temporal masking

Goal: Quantify how a masker sound elevates detection threshold of a brief target.

Protocol:

(1) Present a masker noise (bandpassed or clicks) before (forward) or after (backward) a short tone.
(2) Use 2AFC: target may appear with or without masker; observer indicates presence.
(3) Vary masker–target interval or masker level to measure threshold shift.

Gap Detection

Goal: Probe temporal resolution by finding the shortest silent gap detectable in noise.

Protocol:

(1) Present a noise burst containing a silent gap of duration g in one of two intervals.
(2) 2AFC: observer chooses which interval had the gap.
(3) Staircase adjusts g to converge on 75.

These paradigms – threshold audiometry, frequency discrimination, masking, and gap detection – allow researchers to characterize detection limits, frequency resolution, temporal acuity, and the effects of interference on hearing, providing a comprehensive picture of auditory function.

By combining detailed anatomical knowledge with psychophysical methods – pure-tone audiometry, frequency discrimination, masking, and temporal resolution tests – auditory research maps how we detect, discriminate, and localize sounds in our environment.

2.5 Touch (Somatosensation)

The somatosensory system allows us to perceive mechanical, thermal, and nociceptive (pain) stimuli, as well as proprioceptive signals about limb position and movement [50, 28].

2.5.1 Anatomy and receptor types

In the skin and underlying tissues, specialized receptors transduce different stimulus modalities:

- **Mechanoreceptors:**
  - *Meissner's corpuscles*: rapidly adapting, respond to low-frequency flutter (30–50 Hz), high spatial resolution.
  - *Pacinian corpuscles*: rapidly adapting, tuned to high-frequency vibration (200–300 Hz), detect fine texture.
  - *Merkel disks*: slowly adapting, signal sustained pressure and edges, high spatial discrimination.
  - *Ruffini endings*: slowly adapting, respond to skin stretch and hand shape.
- **Thermoreceptors:** separate warm and cold fibers responding to temperature changes.
- **Nociceptors:** free nerve endings signaling noxious mechanical, thermal, or chemical stimuli.
- **Proprioceptors:** muscle spindles and Golgi tendon organs in muscles and tendons, encode limb position and force.

2.5.2 Neural pathways

Receptor afferents travel via dorsal root ganglia into the spinal cord, ascend in the dorsal columns to the *cuneate* and *gracile* nuclei, cross in the *medulla*, and project through the *medial lemniscus* to the ventral posterior lateral (VPL) thalamus, then to the primary somatosensory cortex (S1).

2.5.3 Key psychophysical paradigms

Two-point discrimination

Purpose: Measure the smallest distance at which two simultaneous skin touches are perceived as separate.

Protocol:

(1) Apply two caliper points at varying separations.
(2) Subject reports "one" or "two" points.
(3) Threshold is the minimum distance for ≥75% correct "two" responses.

Vibrotactile frequency discrimination

Purpose: Determine the smallest detectable difference in vibration frequency on the skin.

Protocol:

(1) Present two sequential vibrations (e.g. 200 Hz vs. 200 Hz + Δf) via a probe.
(2) 2AFC: subject indicates which felt "faster."
(3) Adaptive staircase adjusts Δf to converge on ~75% correct.
(4) Report Weber fraction $\Delta f/f$.

2.5.4 Examples and applications

- Fingertip two-point thresholds ~2 mm (high acuity); forearm 40 mm (low acuity).
- Vibrotactile $\Delta f/f$~0.1–0.2 for frequencies between 50–300 Hz.
- Clinical tests of peripheral neuropathy often use monofilament (von Frey)
- pressure thresholds.

These paradigms, combined with knowledge of receptor types and neural pathways, enable quantitative mapping of tactile sensitivity and spatial resolution across the body surface.

2.6 Taste (Gustation)

Taste, or gustation, arises when dissolved chemicals interact with specialized receptors in taste buds of the tongue and oral cavity [53]. The five primary taste qualities – sweet, sour, salty, bitter, and umami – are encoded by distinct receptor mechanisms. After transduction, signals travel via cranial nerves (VII, IX, X) to the nucleus of the solitary tract (NTS), then thalamus, and finally to primary gustatory cortex in the insula and frontal operculum.

2.6.1 Anatomy and receptor mechanisms

- **Papillae types:** *Fungiform* (anterior tongue), *foliate* (lateral), *circumvallate* (posterior). Each contains 100–300 taste buds.
- **Receptor cells:**
  1. *Ion channels* (salt: ENaC; sour: PKD2L1).
  2. *G-protein-coupled receptors* (sweet: T1R2/T1R3; umami: T1R1/T1R3; bitter: 25 T2Rs).

2.6.2 Neural pathway

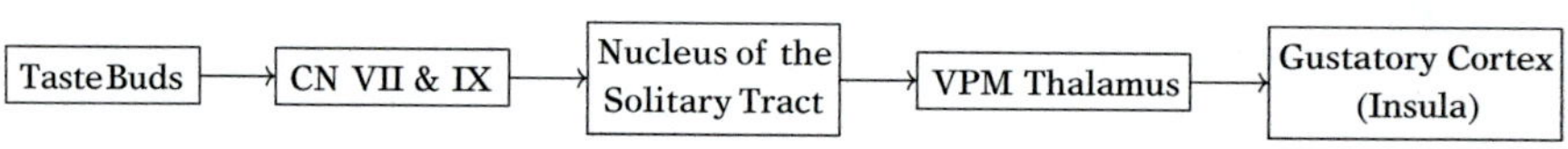

2.6.3 Key psychophysical paradigms

Detection thresholds (method of limits)

Goal: Find the lowest concentration at which a taste quality is reliably detected.

Protocol:

(1) Prepare serial dilutions of a tastant (e.g. NaCl for salt).
(2) Present ascending and descending concentrations, rinsing mouth between.
(3) Observer indicates "Yes/No" for detection.
(4) Threshold is mean "crossover" concentration.

Recognition thresholds (constant stimuli)

Goal: Determine concentration at which taste quality is correctly identified (e.g. "sweet").

Protocol:

(1) Present randomized samples across concentrations.
(2) Observer labels taste (forced-choice among five qualities).
(3) Plot percent correct vs. concentration; read 75% point.

2.6.4 Examples and applications

- **Sweet sensitivity:** Detection threshold 10 mM sucrose.
- **Bitter sensitivity:** Variation due to TAS2R38 genotype – "tasters" vs. "non-tasters."
- **Cross-modal interactions:** Aroma can enhance perceived sweetness – used in food industry to reduce sugar.

By combining anatomical insights with psychophysical methods, we can quantitatively map taste sensitivity, discrimination, and flavor perception across individuals and populations.

2.7 Smell (olfaction)

Olfaction allows us to detect and discriminate thousands of volatile chemical compounds. Olfactory receptor neurons in the nasal epithelium express ~ one of ~400 odorant receptor (OR) genes [46]. Their axons converge onto glomeruli in the olfactory bulb, which relays a topographic odor map to primary olfactory (piriform) cortex and higher areas.

2.7.1 Anatomy and receptor mechanisms

- **Olfactory epithelium:** Located in the superior nasal cavity, contains
  1. *Olfactory receptor neurons (ORNs)* with cilia bearing OR proteins.
  2. *Supporting (sustentacular) cells.*
  3. *Basal (stem) cells* that regenerate ORNs.

- **Receptor families:** Each ORN expresses one OR gene; ORs are G- protein coupled receptors that, upon binding an odorant, activate an adenylate cyclase cascade → cAMP → opens cation channels → depolarization.

Figure 2.12 Simplified olfactory pathway: odorants activate receptor neurons in the epithelium, converge in the bulb's glomeruli, and project to piriform cortex.

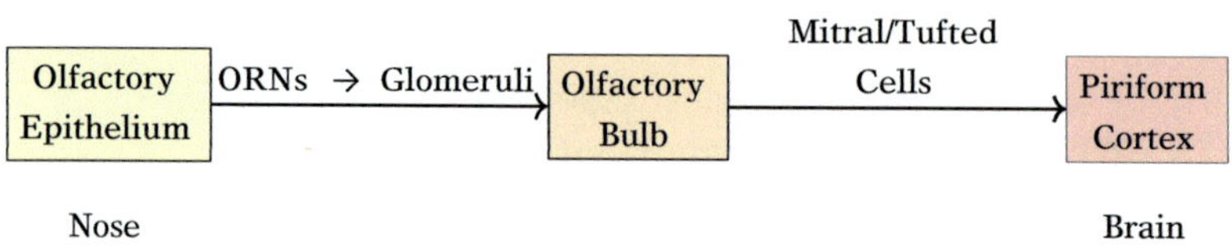

2.7.2 Neural pathways

- ORN axons pass through the cribriform plate to glomeruli in the olfactory bulb.
- *Mitral* and *tufted* cells relay to piriform cortex, amygdala, and entorhinal cortex – bypassing thalamus.
- Higher processing in orbitofrontal cortex integrates olfactory with gustatory and somatosensory inputs for flavor.

2.7.3 Key psychophysical paradigms

Detection thresholds

Goal: Find the lowest concentration of an odorant detectable.

Protocol:

(1) Prepare serial dilutions of a standard odor (e.g. phenylethyl alcohol).
(2) Method of limits: ascending/descending presentation via sniff bottles.
(3) Observer reports "Yes/No" to detect odor.
(4) Threshold = mean concentration at crossover.

Discrimination and identification

Odor discrimination (2AFC):

(1) Present two sniff samples, one different odor or concentration.
(2) Observer chooses which differs.
(3) Staircase yields Δ concentration or mixture ratio JND.

Odor identification:

(1) Present single odor; subject picks label from a list.
(2) Measures familiarity and cognitive factors; threshold at percent correct.

2.7.4 Examples and applications

- **Specific anosmia:** ~30% of people cannot detect androstenone due to OR gene variation.
- **Odor mixture perception:** Up to ~4 components can be distinguished in a blend; beyond that perception becomes configural.
- **Clinical testing:** The University of Pennsylvania Smell Identification Test (UPSIT) uses 40 microencapsulated odors in scratch-and-sniff booklets.

Adaptive olfactory testing

Modern olfactometers deliver precise pulses of odorized air; adaptive algorithms adjust concentration in real time to estimate thresholds efficiently, analogous to auditory staircases.

Olfactory psychophysics thus bridges molecular receptor biology with perception and behavior, revealing how we detect, differentiate, and identify the rich world of smells.

2.8 Psychophysics and Developmental Psychology

Understanding how infants perceive and interpret the world around them has been a major milestone in the area of psychophysics. Infants below one year of age have limited motor and language capabilities and so psychophysics experiments have relied on non-verbal methods like the looking-time paradigms which rely on simple, observable behaviors like looking. They help us answer fundamental questions: How do infants see, hear, and understand the world? How early do they form concepts, make predictions, or learn associations? And how do these abilities change over time – or fail to develop in certain conditions? These experimental paradigms continue to be integral part of modern infant research, offering an indirect yet powerful window into the infant mind. When combined with psychophysical methods – the quantitative study of the relationship between physical stimuli and perceptual responses – looking-time measures allow researchers to precisely investigate sensory and perceptual thresholds, discrimination abilities, and early cognitive processes.

Definition 7: Developmental psychology. The study of how cognitive, emotional, and perceptual abilities evolve across the lifespan, from infancy through old age.

2.8.1 Historical foundations: The work of Robert Fantz

The pioneering work of Robert Fantz (1964) became a turning point in infant perception research with the introduction of the *preferential looking paradigm* (PLP) [10]. In his landmark 1964 study, Fantz demonstrated that infants as young as two months old exhibited *spontaneous visual preferences.* Using a "looking chamber," Fantz presented infants with two visual stimuli side-by- side – a patterned stimulus (e.g., a checkerboard or face) and a blank one – and found that infants consistently looked longer at the patterned image. Infants looking longer at the patterned stimulus indicates that they are able to discriminate between the stimuli and preferred one over the other.

This simple and elegant technique of presenting infants with two stimuli side-by-side (e.g., a patterned checkerboard and a plain disk), provided the first empirical evidence that infants possess *innate perceptual preferences.* The visual preference indicated that infants do not attend to all visual stimuli equally; rather, they show consistent preferences – looking longer at patterns, faces, or novel stimuli over blank or familiar ones. This early work by Fantz laid the foundation for a wide range of research methodologies in developmental psychophysics, enabling researchers to ask increasingly nuanced questions about infant perception, attention, memory, and cognition, including language. Consequently, *looking-time measures* have emerged as one of the most widely used and foundational tools for studying the emergence of perceptual, attentional, and cognitive processes in early life.

The *preferential looking paradigm (PLP)* was revolutionary because it provided a *non-invasive, behavior-based measure of visual discrimination and interest*. Thus, Fantz's work laid a strong foundation for pioneering research into perceptual and cognitive development by establishing that infants are active processors of sensory information, capable of preference, attention, and learning.

2.8.2 Infant looking paradigms in psychophysical research

When combined with psychophysical methods, infant looking paradigms provide a powerful lens to quantify and model infant perception with remarkable precision. As technologies improve and theories of development become more nuanced, infant looking paradigms will continue to shape our understanding of the origins of human cognition. Infant looking paradigms are among the most important methodological innovations that allow researchers to probe into a wide range of cognitive, perceptual, and social processes. The basic concept of measuring infant gaze diversified across several key paradigms and has become central to both experimental and clinical research.

(1) **Preferential looking paradigm (PLP).** Infants are presented with two stimuli (simultaneously or sequentially). Infants are familiarized with the stimulus for a fixed amount of time (familiarization). Looking times to test trials and familiarization trials are recorded – either manually or with eye-tracking technology. A visual recovery score of differences in looking times between the test trial and familiarization trial indicates a consistent preference for one stimulus (longer looking). It implies the infant can discriminate between the trials and may find one more interesting, familiar, or novel. Used extensively in studies of *face perception, object recognition, social cognition, and phonetic discrimination.*

(2) **Habituation–dishabituation paradigm.** Infants are repeatedly shown a stimulus until their looking time declines (habituation). A new stimulus is then presented; if looking time increases (dishabituation), it suggests the infant perceives the new stimulus as different. This paradigm is widely used to investigate *categorization, memory, language processing, word learning,* and *numerical cognition.*

(3) **Visual paired comparison (VPC) paradigm.** During the test phase, infants view both a familiar stimulus (from the habituation phase) and a novel one. A preference for the novel stimulus indicates recognition memory and perceptual discrimination. VPC has been used to study *infant memory*, especially in longitudinal studies examining early markers of cognitive impairments.

(4) **Violation-of-expectation (VoE) paradigm.** Infants are shown events that either conform to or violate basic physical, numerical, or social expectations (e.g., object permanence, quantity conservation). Increased looking time at the "impossible" event is interpreted as surprise, indicating that the infant had formed an expectation based on prior knowledge. This paradigm has been instrumental in studying *early physical reasoning, social evaluation*, and *moral development*.

(5) **High-amplitude sucking paradigm (HAS).** Infants are fitted with a specially designed pacifier that contains a pressure transducer to detect changes in sucking amplitude and rate. Infants undergo a baseline phase where their natural sucking rate is recorded to establish an individualized threshold for "high-amplitude" sucks. During the familiarization (habituation) phase, a stimulus (e.g., a speech sound or tone) is presented contingent on high-amplitude sucking – i.e., the infant controls stimulus onset through their sucking behavior. Once the sucking rate decreases to a set habituation criterion (e.g., 50% of the peak rate), a novel stimulus is introduced in the test (dishabituation) phase. An increase in sucking rate in response to the novel stimulus indicates discrimination – the infant perceives the new stimulus as different. This paradigm is used extensively in studies of speech perception, auditory discrimination, language learning, and early categorization, especially in newborns and pre-verbal infants.

(6) **Mobile conjugate reinforcement paradigm (MCRP).** Infants (typically 2–6 months old) are placed in a crib with a ribbon tied to one of their ankles. The other end of the ribbon is connected to a mobile suspended above the crib, allowing the infant's leg movements to cause the mobile to move (conjugate reinforcement). Baseline phase: infant's spontaneous kicking rate is recorded without the mobile moving to establish a baseline level of activity. Learning (reinforcement) phase: the ribbon is attached to the mobile so that each kick causes the mobile to move. The infant learns the contingency between their kicking and the mobile's motion. Retention test (after a delay of hours or days): infant is placed back in the crib with the ribbon connected but the mobile is either present or absent, and the kicking rate is recorded again to assess memory of the contingency. An increased kicking rate compared to baseline indicates learning and memory retention – the infant remembers that kicking causes the mobile to move. This is used to assess learning, memory retention over time, contextual effects, and the emergence of long-term memory in preverbal infants [39].

It is obvious from all of these paradigms that the fundamental principles of psychophysics described in previous chapters are used to determine the relationship between the properties of physical stimuli (e.g., brightness, contrast, pitch) and the perceptual responses they elicit. In adults, psychophysics often involves subjective reports, button presses, or scaling tasks. In infants, however, researchers must infer perception from observable behaviors – primarily looking. Here are a few examples:

(1) **Visual acuity and contrast sensitivity.** *Teller acuity cards* and similar tools present striped patterns (gratings) on one side of a card, with varying spatial frequencies. An experimenter, blind to the location of the stripes, observes the infant's gaze direction to infer whether the

pattern is visible. By systematically varying the spatial frequency or contrast, researchers can estimate an infant's *visual acuity* or *contrast sensitivity function.* These techniques reveal that *newborns have limited acuity,* which improves rapidly in the first year of life.

(2) **Depth and motion perception.** *Looming stimuli* (objects increasing in size to simulate approach) are used to measure defensive blinking or increased looking as cues of depth and motion. The *kinetic depth* effect and *motion parallax* cues are also tested by presenting rotating or moving objects in 3D. Preferential looking to dynamic vs. static stimuli indicates developing *motion sensitivity* and *binocular depth perception.*

(3) **Color discrimination and perception.** By habituating infants to a specific wavelength and presenting new ones, researchers assess the ability to distinguish between hues. Studies using looking-time paradigms have shown that *color categories* (e.g., red vs. green) can be perceived by 3–4 months of age, suggesting early development of trichromatic vision. This method has been key to understanding the *ontogeny of color vision* and *cross-cultural studies of color categorization.*

(4) **Auditory–visual integration.** In experiments assessing *multisensory integration,* infants are presented with visual and auditory stimuli simultaneously. For example, they may watch two faces mouthing different syllables while hearing one of them – infants often look longer at the matching (congruent) face. These studies suggest that even young infants are capable of *cross-modal matching,* important for early *language acquisition* and *social cognition.*

Developmental critical periods

During early infancy (0–6 months), deprivation (e.g. congenital cataract) can permanently alter contrast sensitivity. Timely intervention (e.g. cataract removal) within this "critical period" is essential for normal visual development.

Key takeaways

- *Ontogeny of thresholds:* Sensory sensitivity follows nonlinear developmental trajectories.
- *Critical periods:* Early experience can have lasting effects on perceptual systems.
- *Plasticity persists:* Psychophysical training and exposure continue to shape perception into adulthood.

2.8.3 Technological advances in infant looking studies

In recent years, eye-tracking technology has significantly enhanced the precision of looking-time paradigms. While traditional methods relied on experimenter observation or video coding, modern eye-trackers can:

- Measure fixation duration, saccades, and pupil dilation.
- Detect subtle shifts in attention within milliseconds.
- Allow for real-time presentation of contingent stimuli, increasing experimental control and ecological validity.

Eye-tracking has enabled more fine-grained analyses of infant attention patterns and facilitated new experimental designs involving gaze-contingent learning, anticipatory looking, and temporal dynamics of information processing.

2.9 Example PsychoPy Experiment: A Working Memory Sequence–Judgement Task

In this experiment, observers view a brief sequence of colored squares (set size 2, 4, 6, or 8) presented one at a time at random locations on an imaginary circle. After a short retention interval, two of the previously seen items reappear side by side, and the participant must judge either which appeared *first* (primacy) or which appeared *last* (recency). Accuracy and reaction time (RT) are recorded on each trial.

Key concepts

Serial position effects

Memory for list items typically shows a *primacy effect* (better recall of early items) and a *recency effect* (better recall of late items). By probing either the earliest or latest item in the sequence, this task quantifies how these effects vary with set size and modality.

Cognitive load and set size

As set size increases, working memory capacity is taxed, leading to decreased accuracy and longer RTs. Plotting performance (accuracy vs. set size) reveals the functional limit of visual working memory (often around 4 ± 1 items).

Psychophysical considerations

- **Controlled timing:** Each square appears for 800 ms, with a 200 ms inter-stimulus interval (jittered), ensuring uniform encoding time.
- **Random spatial positions**: By randomizing presentation locations on a circle (radius 150 px) and shuffling order, spatial and order cues are decorrelated.
- **Response mapping:** LEFT versus RIGHT arrows map onto "earlier" or "later" judgments; counterbalanced across trials to prevent motor bias.

Data analysis concepts

- **Accuracy curves:** Plot percent correct vs. set size, separately for primacy and recency judgments.
- **Reaction time (RT):** Analyze mean RT as a function of set size and judgment type to assess processing speed and decision difficulty.
- **Serial position profiles:** Examine accuracy for different probe positions (first vs. last vs. middle) to characterize the shape of primacy/recency effects.

This paradigm probes the limits of visual working memory and reveals how encoding strength and retrieval order interact in human cognition.

Figure 2.13 Illustration of the random circular layout: items appear one by one at equidistant angular positions, but presentation order is randomized.

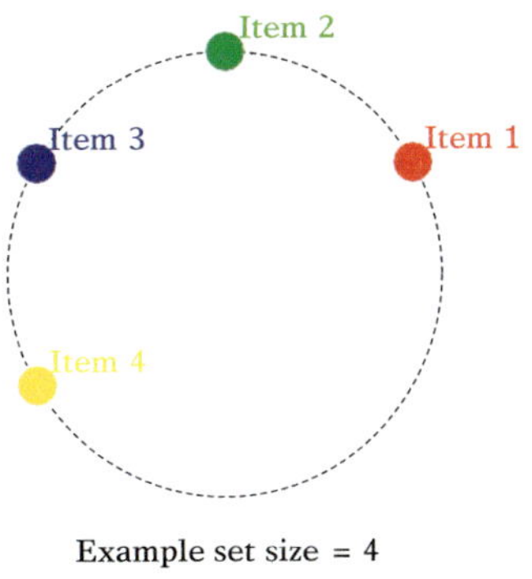

2.9.1 Experiment code

Listing 2.1 PsychoPy Experiment Script

```
from PsychoPy import visual, core, event # Import PsychoPy modules
import random, math, csv

# --- Experiment Setup ---
# Create a window (adjust size/fullscreen as needed)
win = visual.Window(size=[800, 600], units='pix', fullscr=False, color=[0, 0, 0])

# Define a list of 8 easily distinguishable RGB colors
colors = [
    [1, 0, 0], # Red
    [0, 1, 0], # Green
    [0, 0, 1], # Blue
    [1, 1, 0], # Yellow
    [1, 0, 1], # Magenta
    [0, 1, 1], # Cyan
    [0.5, 0.5, 0.5], # Gray
    [1, 0.5, 0] # Orange
]

# Define set sizes and create trial list
set_sizes = [2, 4, 6, 8]
trials = []
# For each set size, create 40 trials with a random judgement type.
for set_size in set_sizes:
    for _ in range(10):
        judgement = random.choice(['recency', 'primacy'])
        trials.append({'set_size': set_size, 'judgement': judgement})
random.shuffle(trials) # Shuffle the overall trial order

# List to store trial data
results = []

# --- Instructions ---
instruction_text = visual.TextStim(win, text="Press any key to start the experiment", color=[1, 1, 1], height=24)
```

```
instruction_text.draw()
win.flip()
event.waitKeys()

# --- Trial Loop ---
for trial in trials:
    set_size = trial['set_size']
    judgement = trial['judgement']

    # Prepare the list of colors for this trial.
    # random.sample returns a list in random order.
    trial_colors = random.sample(colors, set_size)

    # Determine positions on a circle (radius = 150 px).
    # First compute equidistant positions along a circle with a random rotation.
    rotation_offset = random.uniform(0, 360)
    positions = []
    for n in range(set_size):
        angle_deg = rotation_offset + n * (360.0 / set_size)
        angle_rad = math.radians(angle_deg)
        x = 150 * math.cos(angle_rad)
        y = 150 * math.sin(angle_rad)
        positions.append((x, y))
    # Randomize the order in which positions are used so the sequence is not strictly clockwise.
    random.shuffle(positions)

    # Show a fixation cross before the sequence
    fixation = visual.TextStim(win, text="+", color=[1, 1, 1], height =40)
    fixation.draw()
    win.flip()
    core.wait(0.5)

    # Present the sequence one item at a time.
    # The order of presentation is the order of trial_colors, but each is shown at a randomly assigned position.
    for idx, (color_val, pos) in enumerate(zip(trial_colors, positions)):
        square = visual.Rect(win, width=50, height=50, fillColor= color_val, lineColor=color_val, pos=pos)
        square.draw()
        win.flip()
```

```
            core.wait(0.8) # Duration for each square
            win.flip() # Clear the screen
            core.wait(0.2) # Inter-stimulus interval

        # --- Judgement Phase ---
        # Randomly select two distinct indices from the sequence.
        indices = random.sample(range(set_size), 2)
        # Identify which one was presented earlier and which later.
        early = min(indices)
        late = max(indices)

        # Randomly assign the two selected items to the left/right positions.
        if random.choice([True, False]):
            left_index = indices[0]
            right_index = indices[1]
        else:
            left_index = indices[1]
            right_index = indices[0]

        # Record the serial positions (1-indexed) of the items shown at left and right.
        serial_pos_left = left_index + 1
        serial_pos_right = right_index + 1

        # Determine correct answer based on judgement type.
        # For recency, the correct answer is the item that was presented later (i.e. with index == late).
        # For primacy, the correct answer is the item that was presented earlier (i.e. with index == early).
        if judgement == 'recency':
            correct_side = 'left' if left_index == late else 'right'
            question = "Which square appeared later? Left or Right?"
        else: # primacy
            correct_side = 'left' if left_index == early else 'right'
            question = "Which square appeared first? Left or Right?"

        # Display the two squares on left and right sides.
        left_square = visual.Rect(win, width=50, height=50,
                                  fillColor=trial_colors[left_index],
                                  lineColor=trial_colors[left_index],
                                  pos=(-150, 0))
```

```
    right_square = visual.Rect(win, width=50, height=50,
                               fillColor=trial_colors[right_index],
                               lineColor=trial_colors[right_index],
                               pos=(150, 0))
    question_text = visual.TextStim(win, text=question, pos=(0, -200), color=[1, 1, 1], height=24)

    left_square.draw()
    right_square.draw()
    question_text.draw()
    win.flip()

    # Collect response and measure reaction time (RT)
    resp_clock = core.Clock()
    keys = event.waitKeys(keyList=['left', 'right'])
    RT = resp_clock.getTime() * 1000 # Convert seconds to milliseconds
    response = keys[0]

    # Determine response accuracy
    accuracy = 1 if response == correct_side else 0

    # Save trial results, including the serial positions of the probed items.
    results.append({
        'set_size': set_size,
        'judgement': judgement,
        'accuracy': accuracy,
        'RT': RT,
        'probe_serial_left': serial_pos_left,
        'probe_serial_right': serial_pos_right
    })

    # Inter-trial interval: clear screen
    win.flip()
    core.wait(0.5)

# Save data to a CSV file
with open('data.csv', 'w', newline='') as csvfile:
    fieldnames = ['set_size', 'judgement', 'accuracy', 'RT', ' probe_serial_left', 'probe_serial_right']
    writer = csv.DictWriter(csvfile, fieldnames=fieldnames)
```

```
        writer.writeheader()
        for row in results:
            writer.writerow(row)


# --- End of Experiment ---
thanks = visual.TextStim(win, text="Thank you for participating!",
    color=[1, 1, 1], height=24)
thanks.draw()
win.flip()
core.wait(2)

win.close()
core.quit()
```

2.9.2 Running the experiment

To run the experiment:

(1) Open PsychoPy and switch to the Coder view.
(2) Create a new script and paste the above code.
(3) Save the script as serial men.py.
(4) Click the green "Run" button or press F5 to execute the script.
(5) After completing the trials, a CSV file will be saved in the same directory.

2.9.3 Data analysis in Google Colab

After collecting data, you can analyze it using Google Colab:

(1) Upload the csv to your Colab environment.
(2) Run the following Python code to compute and plot the psychometric function:

Listing 2.2 Data Analysis in Google Colab

```
import pandas as pd
import numpy as np
import matplotlib.pyplot as plt
from scipy.stats import sem # For standard error computation

```

```
# === Load the Data ===
# Adjust the filename if necessary.
data = pd.read_csv(’data.csv’)

# === Compute Descriptive Statistics ===
# Group by set_size and judgement (primacy or recency) and compute :
# - count: number of trials
# - mean and standard deviation of accuracy
# - mean and standard deviation of RT (in ms)
group_stats = data.groupby([’set_size’, ’judgement’]).agg(
    count=(’accuracy’, ’count’),
    mean_accuracy=(’accuracy’, ’mean’),
    std_accuracy=(’accuracy’, ’std’),
    mean_RT=(’RT’, ’mean’),
    std_RT=(’RT’, ’std’)
).reset_index()

# Compute the standard error of the mean (SEM) for accuracy and RT.
group_stats[’sem_accuracy’] = group_stats[’std_accuracy’] / np.
    sqrt(group_stats[’count’])
group_stats[’sem_RT’] = group_stats[’std_RT’] / np.sqrt( group_stats[’count’])

# Print the descriptive statistics table.
print(“Descriptive Statistics by Set Size and Judgement:”)
print(group_stats)
    group_stats.to_csv(’descriptive_statistics.csv’)

# === Plotting Average Accuracy by Set Size ===
# This figure shows the average accuracy (with error bars representing SEM)
# for each set size, separated by judgement type.
fig, ax = plt.subplots(figsize=(8, 6))
judgements = data[’judgement’].unique()

for jud in judgements:
    # Filter statistics for this judgement type.
    sub_df = group_stats[group_stats[’judgement’] == jud]
    ax.errorbar(sub_df[’set_size’], sub_df[’mean_accuracy’], yerr=
        sub_df[’sem_accuracy’],
                marker=’o’, capsize=5, label=jud)

```

```
ax.set_title('Set Size Wise Average Accuracy')
ax.set_xlabel('Set Size')
ax.set_ylabel('Average Accuracy')
ax.legend()
 plt.tight_layout()
 plt.savefig('analysis_results.png',    dpi=300)
plt.show()

# === Plotting Mean Reaction Time (RT) by Set Size ===
# This figure shows the mean RT (in milliseconds) with SEM error bars,
# separately for primacy and recency judgement trials.
fig, ax = plt.subplots(figsize=(8, 6))
for jud in judgements:
    sub_df = group_stats[group_stats['judgement'] == jud]
    ax.errorbar(sub_df['set_size'], sub_df['mean_RT'], yerr=sub_df ['sem_RT'],
                marker='o', capsize=5, label=jud)

ax.set_title('Set Size Wise Mean Reaction Time (RT)')
ax.set_xlabel('Set Size')
ax.set_ylabel('Mean RT (ms)')
ax.legend()
plt.tight_layout()
plt.savefig('analysis_results_RT.png', dpi=300)
plt.show()
```

2.10 Student Exercises

(1) **ITD and ILD cues.** Calculate the maximum interaural time difference (ITD) for a head diameter of 18 cm, assuming sound travels at 343 m/s. Describe how ITD and ILD cues would interact to localize a broadband noise source at 30° to the right.

(2) **Weber–Fechner vs. Stevens' power law.** For light intensity I, compare predicted perceived sensation S under Fechner's law ($S = k \ln I$) and Stevens' power law ($S = kI^{0.33}$). Choose $k = 1$ and plot both functions for I from 1 to 100. Which law better accounts for very dim stimuli?

(3) **Two-point discrimination.** Design a two-point discrimination experiment for fingertip skin: specify stimulus apparatus, set of separations to test, and a method (limits, constant stimuli, or adjustment). Describe how you would estimate the discrimination threshold and control for response bias.

(4) **Olfactory adaptation.** Propose a simple psychophysical protocol to measure adaptation to a citrus odor: how would you quantify the decrease in perceived intensity over time, and how would you account for individual differences in baseline sensitivity?

2.11 Additional Reading

- Goldstein, E. B. (2018). *Sensation and Perception* (10th ed.). Cengage Learning. A comprehensive introduction to the major sensory systems, with chapters on visual, auditory, somatosensory, gustatory, and olfactory Psychophysics.
- Kingdom, F. A. A., & Prins, N. (2016). *Psychophysics: A Practical Introduction* (2nd ed.). Academic Press. A hands-on guide to designing and analyzing psychophysical experiments across modalities.
- Yantis, S., & Saffran, J. (2020). "Development of the Senses" in *Developmental Psychology* (3rd ed.), Chapter 5. Wiley. Explores how sensory systems mature over the lifespan and the interplay between Psychophysics and developmental processes.
- Fantz, R. L. (1964). Visual experience in infants: Decreased attention to familiar patterns relative to novel ones. *Science*, 146(3644), 668–670.
- Rovee-Collier, C., Hartshorn, K., & DiRubbo, M. (1999). Long-term maintenance of infant memory. *Developmental Psychobiology: The Journal of the International Society for Developmental Psychobiology*, 35(2), 91–102.

CHAPTER

3

Signal Detection Theory and Experimental Design

3.1 Introduction to Psychophysical Methods

Psychophysics is the scientific study of the relationship between physical stimuli and the sensations and perceptions they produce. As such, psychophysics plays a central role in understanding how we experience the world through our senses. This chapter introduces the foundational experimental methods used in psychophysics and outlines key concepts that are essential for designing, conducting, and interpreting perceptual experiments [6].

3.1.1 The scientific method in psychophysics

Like all empirical sciences, psychophysics relies on a scientific method to answer questions about human perception. This method involves:

(1) **Formulating a hypothesis:** For example, "Do people perceive a higher- pitched tone as louder than a lower-pitched tone, even when they are physically equal in amplitude?"
(2) **Designing an experiment:** This includes selecting appropriate stimuli, determining how responses will be measured, and controlling extraneous factors.
(3) **Collecting data systematically:** Using controlled presentations of stimuli and recording participant responses (e.g., yes/no, forced choice, ratings, reaction time).
(4) **Analyzing results:** Applying statistical tools to determine if observed patterns support or refute the hypothesis.
(5) **Drawing conclusions and revising theories:** Results may confirm, refine, or challenge existing models of sensory processing.

DOI: 10.1201/9788743809456-3

3.1.2 Experimental variables

Every experiment involves different types of variables, and clear understanding of their roles is crucial:

- **Independent variable (IV):** This is the variable that the experimenter manipulates. In psychophysics, this often includes properties of the stimulus such as brightness, frequency, duration, or spatial location.
- **Dependent variable (DV):** This is what the experimenter measures in response to changes in the IV. In psychophysical studies, common dependent variables include accuracy, reaction time (RT), or subjective ratings of intensity.
- **Control variables**: These are aspects of the experiment that are held constant to ensure that changes in the DV are due to the IV alone. Examples include background lighting, viewing distance, and timing parameters.

Understanding and clearly identifying these variables helps researchers draw meaningful conclusions from their experiments.

3.1.3 Validity and reliability

Two fundamental criteria for evaluating psychophysical experiments are validity and reliability:

- **Internal validity** refers to how well the experiment is designed to isolate the relationship between the IV and DV. A study has high internal validity if the observed effects can confidently be attributed to the experimental manipulation, rather than confounding variables.
- **External validity** concerns the generalizability of the findings. Do the results apply only in the lab, or do they extend to real-world conditions? For example, measuring color discrimination on a computer screen may not directly predict behavior in natural lighting.
- **Reliability** refers to the consistency and repeatability of the results. A reliable psychophysical measure yields similar results across repeated trials or sessions. This is particularly important in perceptual threshold estimation, where individual differences and internal noise can influence outcomes.

3.1.4 Key concept: Counterbalancing and randomization

One of the most important tools in psychophysical methodology is the use of counterbalancing and randomization to avoid systematic biases:

- **Counterbalancing** involves systematically varying the order of conditions across participants to control for order effects or practice effects. For example, if two types of stimuli are presented in fixed order, participants might perform better on the second simply due to learning or fatigue. Counterbalancing ensures that such effects do not bias the results.

- **Randomization** refers to the practice of varying the sequence of stimuli or conditions randomly for each participant. This helps to prevent predictable patterns and minimizes biases caused by expectation or habituation.

Together, these methods ensure that the data collected reflect true perceptual responses rather than artifacts of the experimental design.

3.1.5 Applying psychophysical principles to the serial memory experiment

To better understand the key concepts introduced earlier, let's examine how they are reflected in the serial memory experiment from the previous chapter (see Section 2.9.1). This experiment investigates how memory for colors presented in a sequence varies depending on set size and judgment type (recency vs. primacy).

(1) **Scientific method in action.** This experiment follows the scientific method:
  - **Hypothesis:** People may find it harder to judge the order of items as set size increases, and recency judgments might be faster or more accurate than primacy judgments.
  - **Experimental design:** The experiment varies the number of items (2, 4, 6, or 8) and asks participants to make either a recency or primacy judgment.
  - **Data collection:** Reaction time (RT) and accuracy are recorded for each trial, giving insight into memory performance.
  - **Analysis and interpretation:** The results can be analyzed to reveal how set size and judgment type affect memory accuracy and speed.

(2) **Independent, dependent, and control variables.** This experiment includes:
  - **Independent variables (IV):**
    - *Set size* (2, 4, 6, 8 items) – manipulated to observe effects of memory load.
    - *Judgment type (*recency or primacy) – whether the participant is asked which item came later or earlier.
  - **Dependent variables (DV):**
    - *Accuracy* – whether the participant selected the correct item.
    - *Reaction time (RT)* – how long it took to respond, in milliseconds.
  - **Control variables:**
    - *Stimulus properties* – all items are easily distinguishable colors and equal in size.
    - *Display duration* – each square is shown for 0.8 seconds with a 0.2 second interval.
    - *Positioning* – although randomized, positions are equidistant from the center, controlling for spatial factors.

By controlling key aspects of the experiment, researchers can ensure that any differences in performance are likely due to memory demands, not other confounding factors.

(3) **Validity and reliability**

- **Internal validity** is strengthened by the random assignment of colors and positions, as well as randomization of judgment type across trials. This reduces biases that might otherwise influence performance.
- **External validity** is moderate – while the task is artificial (colored squares in circles), it reflects real cognitive demands like remembering sequences, which are common in everyday tasks (e.g., remembering phone numbers or shopping lists).
- **Reliability** is supported by using multiple trials per condition (10 per set size and judgment type), allowing consistent patterns to emerge across participants.

(4) **Counterbalancing and randomization.** These techniques help ensure the results are not biased:

- **Randomization of trial order:** The full list of trials is shuffled so participants do not get used to a pattern of easy or difficult trials.
- **Random assignment of judgement type:** Each trial independently assigns either a recency or primacy task, avoiding predictability.
- **Random color and position assignment:** Colors are sampled without replacement to ensure distinct stimuli, and their positions around the circle are rotated and randomized, minimizing location-based cues.
- **Random probe positioning:** The two probed items are randomly placed on the left and right sides, and their serial positions vary from trial to trial.

These features make it difficult for participants to rely on non-memory strategies, ensuring the task genuinely measures sequence memory. In sum, this serial memory experiment is an example of how core psychophysical principles are applied in real research. It uses design to isolate memory processes, ensuring that the results are meaningful, valid, and scientifically interpretable.

In the sections that follow, we will look into specific psychophysical methods – such as the method of limits, method of constant stimuli, and signal detection theory – and explore how they are applied in real experiments to study perception and cognition.

3.2 Experimental Design Principles

Careful experimental design is essential to draw valid conclusions in psychophysics. Here we compare two major designs and then discuss how to choose an appropriate sample size.

3.2.1 Between-subjects vs. within-subjects designs

Between-subjects design. Different groups of participants experience different conditions (e.g. Group A sees high-contrast stimuli, Group B sees low-contrast).

- *Advantages*: No carryover or practice effects; simpler logistics when testing many conditions.
- *Limitations*: Requires larger total n to achieve the same statistical power; greater variability due to individual differences.

Within-subjects design. The same participants experience all conditions (e.g. each observer performs trials at high and low contrast).

- *Advantages*: Controls for inter-individual variability; increased statistical power with fewer subjects.
- *Limitations*: Potential for order, practice, or fatigue effects; requires counterbalancing.

Example: Visual acuity testing

- *Between-subjects*: Two matched groups tested on either high-resolution or low-resolution display.
- *Within-subjects*: Each observer reads charts at multiple resolutions in counterbalanced order.

3.2.2 Sampling methods and power analysis

Sampling methods

- **Simple:** Every participant in the population has equal chance of selection.
- **Stratified sampling:** Population divided into subgroups (e.g. age bands), then randomly sampled within each stratum to ensure representativeness.
- **Convenience sampling:** Uses readily available participants (e.g. students); quick but may limit generalizability.

Power and sample size. Statistical power $(1 - \beta)$ is the probability of detecting a true effect (Figure 3.1). Required sample size n depends on:

$$n = \frac{(Z_{\alpha/2} + Z_{\beta})^2 \cdot \sigma^2}{\delta^2}$$

- $Z_{\alpha/2}$: Critical value for significance level α (e.g., 1.96 for $\alpha = 0.05$)
- Z_{β}: Critical value for power $1 - \beta$ (e.g., 0.84 for 80% power)
- σ : Population standard deviation
- δ : Minimum detectable effect size

For confidence intervals (not power), sample size is:

$$n = \frac{Z_{\alpha/2}\sigma^2}{E}$$

Figure 3.1 Statistical power: probability of correctly rejecting H_0 when H_a is true. Power increases with larger effect size (δ), larger sample size (n), and higher significance level (α).

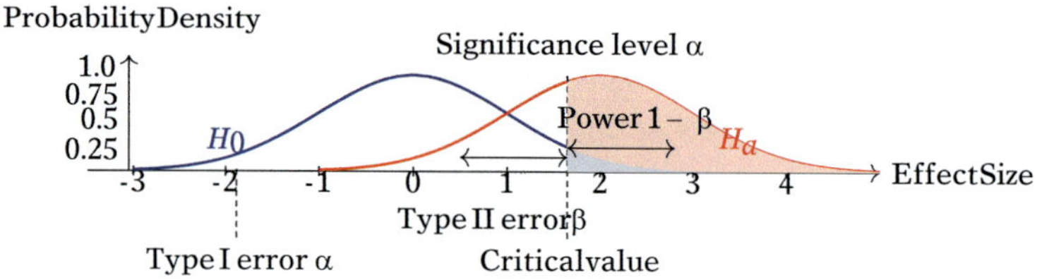

where E is the margin of error.

Important notes:

- For t-tests: Replace Z with t-values (depends on df)
- For proportions: $\sigma = \sqrt{p(1-p)}$
- Use software (G*Power, R, Python) for precise calculations
- Always report power when publishing null results.

Practical tool

G*Power is free software for power analyses across many statistical tests. Input your expected effect size, α, and desired power to compute n.

Example: Confidence interval sample size. For a population mean with σ = 1.0, margin of error E = 0.2, and 95% confidence ($z_{\alpha/2}$ = 1.96, See Figure 3.2):

$$n = \frac{z_{\alpha/2} \cdot \sigma^2}{E} = \frac{1.96 \times 1.0^2}{0.2} = 96.04 \approx 97^{\dagger}$$

†Rounded up to ensure precision. In practice, use n = 97.

Key assumptions: normally distributed data, known σ.

3.2.3 Common experimental pitfalls

Even well-designed psychophysical experiments can be undermined by practical issues that bias results. Below we describe four frequent pitfalls, illustrate them with examples, and offer concrete solutions.

Figure 3.2 Required sample size n for proportion estimation (95% confidence, $\sigma = 1.0$). As margin of error E decreases, required n increases quadratically. Red: $E = 0.1$ requires $n = 385$. Green: $E = 0.2$ requires $n = 97$.

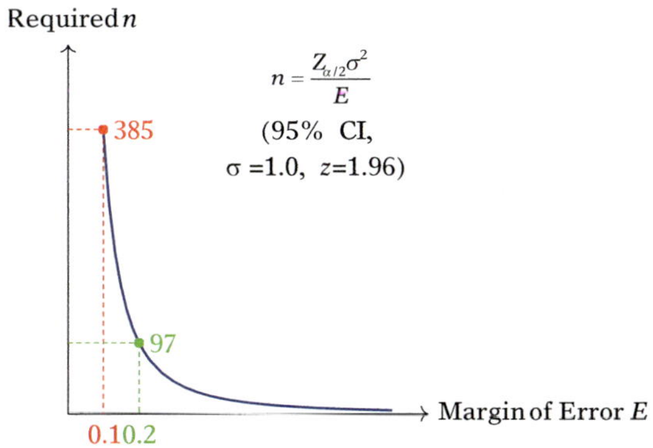

Practice effects

Description: Participants improve simply by repeating the task, confounding learning with the true effect.

Example: In a contrast-detection threshold experiment, subjects may become faster at spotting faint gratings purely through practice, not because contrast sensitivity changed.

Solution:

(1) Counterbalance the order of conditions across participants so learning is distributed evenly.
(2) Include training trials before data collection to reach asymptotic performance.

Fatigue effects

Description: Tiredness or boredom causes performance to deteriorate over long sessions.

Example: In a multi-hour JND experiment, later blocks may show reduced accuracy due to participant fatigue rather than stimulus effects.

Solution:

(1) Limit session length (e.g. 30–45min) and schedule breaks.
(2) Randomize trial order so early and late trials are comparable across conditions.

Demand characteristics

Description: Participants guess the experiment's purpose and alter responses accordingly.

Example: In a taste-intensity study, knowing the goal, subjects might exaggerate "sweetness" ratings for higher concentrations.

Solution:

(1) Use double-blind procedures: both subject and experimenter are unaware of condition labels.
(2) Provide neutral instructions and include catch trials to detect biased responding.

Stimulus order effects

Description: The sequence in which stimuli are presented influences perception (e.g. adaptation or contrast effects)

Example: Presenting very bright stimuli before mid-range ones can raise the threshold for detecting the latter due to light adaptation.

Solution:

(1) Fully randomize stimulus order (method of constant stimuli).
(2) Use balanced Latin-square designs when full randomization is impractical.

3.3 Signal Detection Theory (SDT)

Signal detection theory provides a framework to separate an observer's sensory sensitivity from their decision criterion (bias). It is widely used in psychophysics to analyze detection and discrimination tasks [35, 17, 25, 27].

3.3.1 Core concepts of signal detection theory

Key SDT parameters

Hit rate (H). Probability of correct detection when signal is present (Pr(”yes”|signal)).

False alarm rate (F). Probability of false detection when only noise is present (Pr(”yes”|noise)).

d' **(d-prime).** Sensitivity index: Separation between signal + noise and noise distributions

$$d' = z(H) - z(F) \qquad \text{(in standard deviation units).}$$

β **(beta).** Likelihood ratio criterion: measures response bias

$$\beta = \exp\frac{1}{2}z(F)^2 - z(H)^2$$

ROC curve. Graphical plot of H vs. F showing sensitivity-bias trade- off.

Example: Visual detection experiment

Task*:* Detect a 50 ms light flash at threshold intensity.

(1) **100 noise trials:** no flash presented.
(2) **100 signal trials:** flash presented.

	"Yes"	"No"	Total
Signal trials	75 (hits)	25 (misses)	100
Noise trials	30 (FA)	70 (CR)	100

Calculations:

$$H = 75/100 = 0.75,$$

$$z(H) = \Phi^{-1}(0.75) \approx 0.674$$

$$F = 30/100 = 0.30,$$

$$z(F) = \Phi^{-1}(0.30) \approx -0.524$$

$$d' = z(H) - z(F) = 0.674 - (-0.524) = 1.198$$

$$\beta = \exp \frac{1}{2}\, z(F)^2 - z(H)^2$$

$$= \exp \frac{1}{2}\, (-0.524)^2 - (0.674)^2$$

$$= \exp \frac{1}{2}\, (-0.274576)^2 - (0.454276)^2$$

$$\beta = \exp \frac{1}{2}\, (-0.1797)^2$$

$$= e^{-0.08985} \approx 0.82$$

Interpretation: Moderate sensitivity ($d' \approx 1.2$) with slightly conservative criterion ($\beta < 1$).

Practical considerations

- d' is *response-bias-free*: Only depends on sensitivity.
- β values:
  - $\beta < 1$: Conservative (few "yes" responses)
  - $\beta > 1$: Liberal (many "yes" responses)
  - $\beta = 1$: Neutral bias.
- ROC curves plot H vs. F for different criteria.

Historical context of signal detection theory

Signal detection theory (SDT) has its roots in the 19th century with Gustav 's pioneering work in psychophysics. In his 1860 publication, *Elements of Psychophysics*, he introduced methods to quantify the relationship between physical stimuli and perceived sensations, laying the groundwork for later developments in SDT.

During World War II, the need to improve radar detection systems led engineers and statisticians to develop models to distinguish meaningful signals from background noise. This practical challenge spurred the formalization of SDT concepts, bridging the gap between physical signal processing and human perception [35].

In the 1950s, psychologists such as John A. Swets and David M. Green adapted these principles to the study of human sensory systems. Their work emphasized the role of decision-making processes under uncertainty, introducing key concepts like sensitivity (d') and response bias (β). The publication of *Signal Detection Theory and Psychophysics* in 1966 by Green and Swets solidified SDT's place in psychological research [17].

Today, SDT is a fundamental framework in various fields, including psychology, neuroscience, and medical diagnostics, providing tools to assess perceptual decision-making and the ability to discern signals amidst noise [13].

3.3.2 SDT distributions

Signal detection theory models an observer's internal evidence as arising from two overlapping distributions: one when only noise is present, and one when a signal is added to the noise. The decision criterion c divides the evidence axis – values to the right lead the observer to say "signal present," values to the left to say "signal absent."

Figure 3.3 Gaussian noise (blue) and signal + noise (red) distributions along an internal "evidence" axis. Shaded areas to the right of the criterion c indicate the probabilities of false alarms (blue) and hits (red).

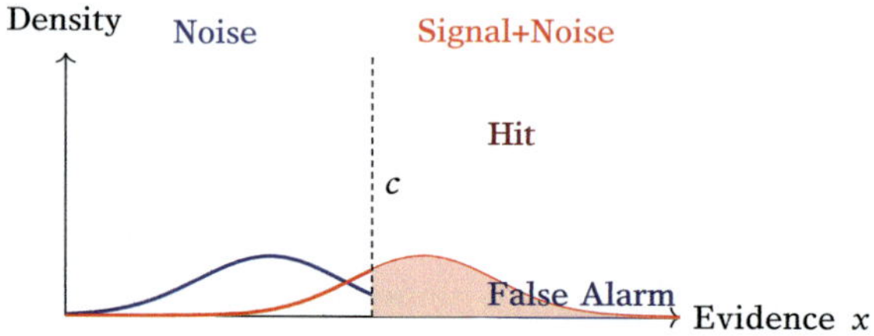

Interpreting hits and false alarms (Figure 3.3)

- **Hit (H):** Evidence $x > c$ on a signal trial. Area under the red curve to the right of c.
- **False alarm (F):** Evidence $x > c$ on a noise trial. Area under the blue curve to the right of c.
- **Miss:** Signal trial but $x \leq c$ (red area left of c).
- **Correct rejection:** Noise trial and $x \leq c$ (blue area left of c).

Example 5: Calculating d' and β). Suppose in a visual detection task you observe $H = 0.84$ and $F = 0.16$. Using standard normal tables:

$$z(H) = 1.0, \qquad z(F) = -1.0 \qquad \Longrightarrow \qquad d' = z(H) - z(F) = 2.0.$$

A neutral criterion ($\beta = 1$) lies midway; a shift of criterion to the right (more conservative) would lower F but also lower H.

3.3.3 ROC curves

The receiver operating characteristic (ROC) curve is a powerful tool in signal detection theory that shows how an observer's sensitivity and decision bias affect performance [49].

In an ROC plot, the false alarm rate (F) is plotted on the x-axis and the hit rate (H) on the y-axis. Each point on the curve corresponds to a different decision criterion – more liberal criteria (saying "yes" more often) result in both higher hits and higher false alarms, while more conservative criteria lower both.

Figure 3.4 shows several ROC curves:

- The diagonal line represents chance performance ($d' = 0$): here, hit and false alarm rates are equal regardless of the criterion.
- The blue curve shows performance at $d' = 1$, a moderate level of sensitivity.
- The red dashed curve shows performance at $d' = 2$, indicating stronger sensitivity and better discrimination between noise and signal.

The more the ROC curve bends toward the upper-left corner (high hit rate, low false alarm rate), the better the observer is at distinguishing signal from noise.

Area under the curve (AUC)

The area under the ROC curve (AUC) is a measure of discriminability.

- AUC = 0.5: chance level ($d' = 0$)
- AUC → 1: perfect discrimination ($d' \to \infty$).

In Figure 3.4 the blue curve has an AUC of 0.76 and the red curve has an AUC of 0.92.

Example 6: Understanding criterion shifts. Imagine you're trying to detect a faint beep in a noisy environment. If you set a *liberal criterion,* you'll report hearing the beep often – you'll catch many actual beeps (high hit rate), but you'll also mistakenly report hearing beeps when there's only noise (high false alarm rate). This moves you up and to the right on the ROC curve.

If you set a *conservative criterion,* you'll only respond "yes" when you're very sure. You'll make fewer false alarms, but you'll also miss some real beeps – moving you down and to the left on the curve.

Key takeaways

- ROC curves help visualize the trade-off between sensitivity (detecting signals) and specificity (avoiding false alarms).
- Different curves represent different levels of d' – the further from the diagonal, the better.
- You can change where you are on a single ROC curve by shifting your decision criterion.

Figure 3.4 Receiver operating characteristic (ROC) curves showing sensitivity levels for $d' = 1$ (AUC = 0.76) and $d' = 2$ (AUC = 0.92). The diagonal represents chance performance ($d' = 0$). Higher d' values curve toward the upper-left corner, indicating better discriminability. The dotted line shows constant response bias.

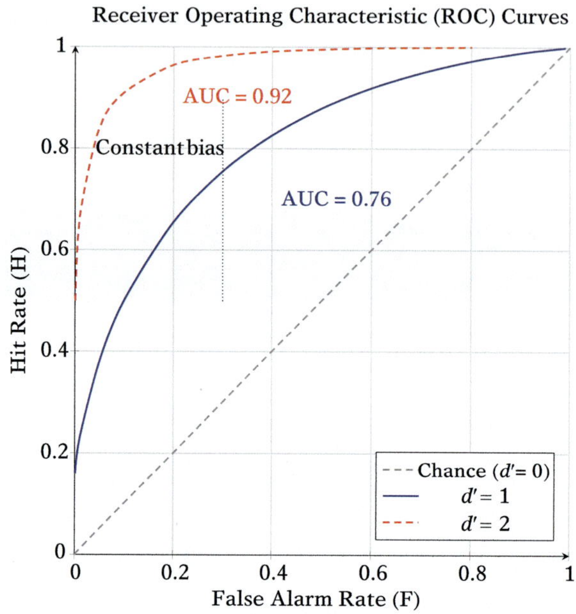

3.3.4 Applying SDT to the brightness discrimination task

In Section 1.8.1 we presented a simple psychophysical experiment in which observers judge whether a single central dot is *darker* or *brighter* than a fixed reference luminance. Here we show how signal detection theory (SDT) concepts map onto that task (Figure 3.5).

Defining signal and noise:

- **Noise trials:** Stimuli with $\Delta L \leq 0$ (dot equal-or-darker than reference).
- **Signal trials:** Stimuli with $\Delta L > 0$ (dot brighter than reference).

Response outcomes:

- **Hit:** Observer presses RIGHT ("brighter") on a signal trial.
- **Miss:** Observer presses LEFT ("darker") on a signal trial.

- **False alarm:** Observer presses RIGHT on a noise trial.
- **Correct rejection:** Observer presses LEFT on a noise trial.

Example confusion matrix

	"Brighter"	"Darker"
Signal ($\Delta L > 0$)	Hit	Miss
Noise ($\Delta L \leq 0$)	False alarm	Correct reject

Estimating sensitivity and bias: After collecting responses for each ΔL, we compute:

$$H = \frac{\#\text{Hits}}{\#\text{Signal trials}}, \qquad F = \frac{\#\text{False Alarams}}{\#\text{Noise trials}}$$

and then

$$d' = z(H) - z(F), \qquad \beta = \exp \frac{1}{2}1\ (z(F)^2 - z(H)^2)\ .$$

Figure 3.5 Idealized SDT model for the brightness task. Noise (darker/equal) and signal (brighter) distributions overlap; the dashed line at *c* is the observer's decision criterion.

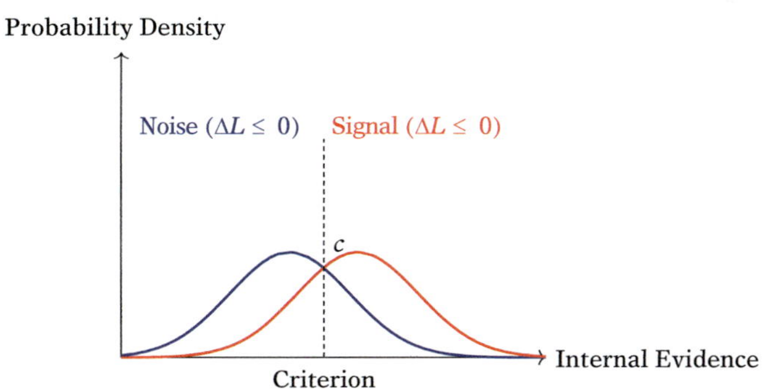

Interpreting results

- A *larger d′* indicates the observer can more reliably distinguish brighter from darker dots (steeper psychometric function).

- The criterion c (or equivalently β) reveals bias:
  - c to the left $\rightarrow$ *liberal* (tendency to say "brighter").
  - c to the right $\rightarrow$ *conservative* (tendency to say "darker").

Practical tip

When hit or false alarm rates are 0 or 1, apply the *log-linear correction*:

$$H' = \frac{H \cdot N_s + 0.5}{N_s + 1}, \qquad F' = \frac{F \cdot N_N + 0.5}{N_N + 1}$$

where N_S and N_N are the numbers of signal and noise trials, respectively.

This mapping of SDT onto our brightness task allows a clean separation of *sensitivity* (how well luminance increments are detected) from *bias* (the observer's tendency to favor one response).

3.3.5 Applications of SDT in psychophysics

Signal detection theory is a versatile framework that extends across many psychophysical domains. Below are four key applications, each illustrated with examples and accompanied by practical tips [59, 17, 35, 18].

1. Sensory threshold measurement

Context: Determining the faintest stimulus an observer can detect (e.g. the lowest sound level, dimmest light, or smallest spice concentration).

SDT approach:

(1) Present near-threshold stimuli interleaved with catch (no- stimulus) trials.
(2) Record hit and false alarm rates.
(3) Compute d' to obtain a bias-free estimate of sensitivity.
(4) Vary stimulus level and chart $d'(L)$ to find the level where $d' \approx 1$ (operational threshold).

Practical tip: Use the *method of constant stimuli* and collect enough catch trials (at least 20%) to reliably estimate false alarms.

2. Memory and recognition

Context: Evaluating how well subjects distinguish old from new items in a recognition memory test.

SDT approach:

(1) Present a study list, then a test list containing old (signal) and new (noise) items.
(2) Ask "Have you seen this item before?" (Yes = signal present).
(3) Compute hit (correct "yes" for old) and false alarm (incorrect "yes" for new) rates.
(4) A high d' indicates strong memory discriminability; criterion shifts reveal response bias (liberal vs. conservative responders).

Example: In word-recognition tasks, older adults often show higher false alarm rates, indicating a shift in criterion rather than reduced sensitivity.

3. Clinical diagnostics

Context: Interpreting medical tests (e.g. mammograms, radiographs) where one must decide if a lesion is present.

SDT approach:

(1) Model healthy images as "noise" and disease-positive images as "signal."
(2) Radiologist's decisions ("disease" vs. "no disease") yield hits and false alarms.
(3) ROC curves summarize performance across criteria (e.g. cost- sensitivity trade-offs).
(4) AUC serves as a single metric of diagnostic accuracy.

Practical tip: Use free-response ROC (FROC) methods for tasks where multiple lesions per image can be marked.

4. Example: Auditory detection in noise

Context: Detecting a tone embedded in background noise – common in hearing research and audiology.

SDT approach:

- Present pure-tone bursts at fixed sound level, interleaved with noise-only trials.
- Observer indicates "tone present" or "absent."
- Compute hit and false alarm rates for each signal-to-noise ratio (SNR).
- Plot ROC curves as SNR varies: curves shift outward as SNR improves.

Across these applications, SDT equips researchers and clinicians with tools to disentangle true sensitivity from decision biases, to compare performance across conditions, and to optimize tasks for maximal discriminability.

3.4 Statistical Analysis Framework

After collecting data from psychophysical experiments, we need appropriate statistical tools to decide whether observed effects are real or could have occurred by chance. Here we briefly review common parametric and non-parametric tests and discuss how to handle multiple comparisons [6].

3.4.1 Parametric tests

After collecting data from psychophysical experiments, one must employ statistical tools to determine whether observed effects reflect true perceptual phenomena or merely chance fluctuations. In this section we provide a concise overview of common parametric and non-parametric tests, as well as strategies for controlling error rates when making multiple comparisons. For a more comprehensive treatment of these methods (including derivations, assumptions, and advanced extensions), please consult a standard statistics textbook such as Howell (2013) or Field et al. (2012).

Key assumptions

(1) **Normality:** Each group's data are approximately normally distributed.
(2) **Homogeneity of variance:** Different groups have similar spread (equal variances).
(3) **Interval data:** Measurements are on a scale where differences are meaningful (e.g. reaction time in ms).

t-Tests:

- **Independent t-test:** Compare means across two *separate* groups (e.g. threshold for Group A vs. Group B).
- **Paired t-test:** Compare means from the *same* participants under two conditions (e.g. pre- vs. post-adaptation).

ANOVA (analysis of variance):

- **One-way ANOVA:** Compare means across more than two groups (e.g. thresholds at three different contrast levels).
- **Factorial ANOVA:** Examine two or more factors (e.g. contrast spatial frequency).
- **Repeated-measures ANOVA:** Like one-way ANOVA but with the same subjects in all conditions.

Example: One-way ANOVA

You test brightness discrimination at low, medium, and high lumi- nance. ANOVA tells you if at least one mean differs significantly, before doing pairwise comparisons.

3.4.2 Non-parametric tests

When parametric assumptions aren't met (e.g. small samples, ordinal data, skewed distributions), non-parametric tests provide robust alternatives.

- **Wilcoxon signed-rank test:** Paired analogue of the paired t-test.
- **Mann–Whitney U test:** Independent analogue of the independent t-test.
- **Friedman test:** Repeated-measures analogue of one-way ANOVA.

When to use non-parametric

- Data are ordinal (e.g. Likert scales).
- Sample size is very small ($n < 10$).
- Distribution is highly skewed or variances differ greatly.

3.4.3 Multiple comparisons problem

Conducting multiple statistical tests increases the chance of a Type I error (false positive).

Family-wise error rate

The probability of making at least one false positive across all tests.

Correction methods:

- **Bonferroni:** Divide your significance threshold α by the number of tests ($\alpha' = \alpha/m$). Simple but conservative.
- **Holm–Bonferroni:** Stepwise method that is less conservative than Bonferroni.
- **False discovery rate (FDR):** Controls expected proportion of false positives among rejected hypotheses.

With these tools in hand, you can choose the appropriate statistical test for your data and control error rates when exploring multiple effects.

3.5 Psychometric Functions

Psychometric functions describe how the probability of a particular response (e.g. "yes, I saw it") depends on stimulus intensity. Fitting a smooth curve to experimental data allows us to estimate key parameters such as threshold and slope [58].

3.5.1 Curve fitting methods

Common choices for the functional form include:

Definition 8: Logistic function. The *logistic* psychometric function is

$$P(x) = \frac{1}{1 + \exp - \frac{x - \mu}{s}},$$

where μ is the threshold (point of 50% performance) and s controls the *slope.*

Definition 9: Weibull function. The *Weibull* function, often used for detection tasks with a non-zero guess rate γ, is

$$W(x) = \gamma + (1 - \gamma)^{h}\, 1 - \exp -(x/\alpha)^{\beta i},$$

where α is the 63% threshold (for $\gamma = 0$), and β controls slope (Figure 3.6).

Figure 3.6 Examples of logistic and Weibull psychometric functions.

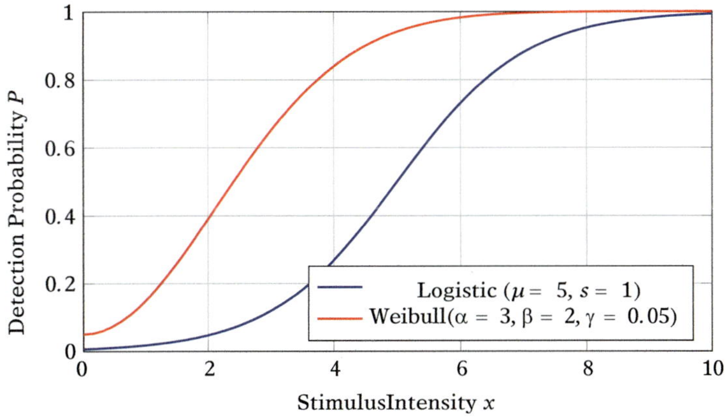

Parameter estimation methods

(1) **Maximum likelihood estimation (MLE):** Finds parameters that maximize the probability of observing the data under the model.

(2) **Bayesian methods:** Combine a prior distribution on parame- ters with the likelihood to obtain a posterior; often use Markov chain Monte Carlo (MCMC).

3.5.2 Threshold estimation

Definition 10. Threshold. The *threshold* is the stimulus intensity x_t corresponding to a specified performance level (e.g. 50%, 75% correct).

- **50% threshold** (μ in logistic) often used for yes/no tasks (Figure 3.7).
- **75% threshold** common in 2AFC tasks, where chance is 50%.

Figure 3.7 Illustration of the 50% (inflection) threshold on a logistic psychometric curve.

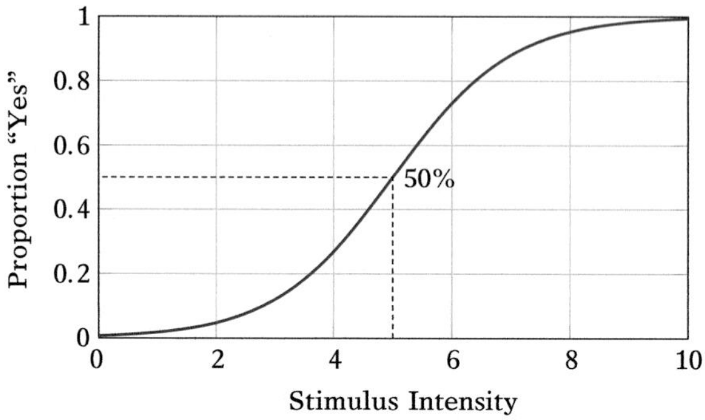

Adaptive methods

Adaptive procedures converge quickly on a threshold:

(1) **QUEST:** Bayesian staircase adjusting stimulus to maintain target performance (e.g. 75%).
(2) **PEST:** Parameter estimation by sequential testing – step size adapts based on previous reversals.

Bootstrap confidence intervals

To quantify uncertainty in threshold estimates:

(1) Resample the data (with replacement) many times.
(2) Refit the psychometric function for each bootstrap sample.
(3) Use the distribution of thresholds to compute, e.g., 95% confidence intervals.

Practical tips:

- Collect at least 50–100 trials across stimulus levels to ensure stable fits.
- Include "catch" trials at extreme intensities to anchor the function's tails.
- Plot data with error bars before fitting to detect anomalies.

3.5.3 Applications of psychometric functions

Psychometric functions are the workhorses of modern psychophysics, linking stimulus intensity to response probability. By fitting an appropriate function to experimental data, one can extract meaningful measures such as detection thresholds, discrimination sensitivity, and response consistency (see Table 3.1 for common psychometric functions and their uses).

Table 3.1 Common applications of psychometric functions in psychophysical tasks.

Task type	Recommended function	Key Measures
Yes/no detection	Logistic or cumulative Gaussian	x50% threshold, slope s, lapse rate λ
Two-alternative Forced-choice (2AFC)	Weibull (with guess rate $\gamma = 0.5$)	x75% threshold, slope β, lapse rate λ
Discrimination (difference limen)	Difference-of-Gaussians or Gumbel	Just-noticeable difference (JND), slope, bias
Rating/confidence judgment	Probit or cumulative normal	Point of subjective equality (PSE), spread σ

- In a *yes/no detection* task, one measures the probability of reporting "yes" as stimulus intensity varies. The 50% point $x_{50\%}$ is taken as the detection threshold.
- In a *2AFC* discrimination task, chance performance is 50%, so one often uses a Weibull fit and defines threshold at 75% correct.
- For *difference limen* tasks, psychometric slopes indicate how sharply performance improves with stimulus differences, yielding the JND.
- *Rating or confidence* tasks use continuous psychometric curves (e.g. probit) to locate the PSE, where two stimuli are judged equal.

Practical note

Always inspect raw proportions with error bars before fitting, choose a function that matches your task's guessing and lapse rates, and report both threshold and slope – together they characterize both sensitivity and precision.

Two-alternative forced-choice (2AFC) task

In a *two-alternative forced-choice* task, on each trial the observer sees (or hears, tastes, etc.) two stimuli – one in each interval or location – and must choose which interval (or side) contains the target or is "stronger." Because there are only two forced options, response bias is minimized: the chance performance level is 50%.

Key points:

(1) *Structure:* Interval 1 vs. Interval 2 (or Left vs. Right). One contains the reference (e.g. baseline intensity), the other a test stimulus (e.g. slightly higher intensity).

(2) *Response:* Participant presses one of two keys (e.g. "1" or "2", "F" or "J") to indicate where the stronger/more intense stimulus appeared.

(3) *Benefits:*

  a. Reduces criterion effects – participant cannot simply say "yes" or "no."
  b. Chance level is known (50%), simplifying sensitivity estimates.

(4) *Analysis:* Plot proportion correct vs. stimulus difference and fit a psychometric curve; threshold often defined at 75% correct (halfway between 50% chance and 100%).

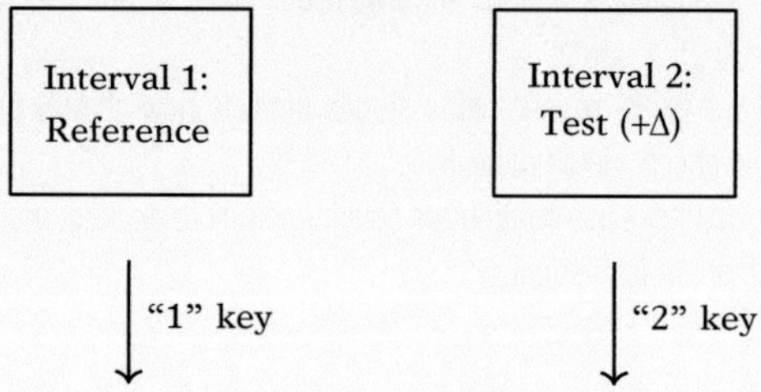

Example: A brightness 2AFC task might present two circles in succession (each for 500 ms), one at a fixed luminance and one slightly brighter. The observer presses "1" if the first was brighter, "2" if the second. By varying the luminance increment and plotting percentage correct, one obtains a psychometric function from which the JND can be estimated.

3.6 Student Exercises

(1) **Design your own psychometric task.** Choose a sensory modality (vision, audition, touch, taste, or smell) and propose a simple yes/no detection experiment. Specify:

- The independent variable(s) and their range of values.
- The dependent measure(s) and how you will record responses.
- Which psychometric function (logistic, Weibull, etc.) you would fit and why.
- How you would estimate threshold and slope from your fitted curve.

(2) **Criterion shifts in SDT.** Simulate (or sketch by hand) how changing the decision criterion *c* affects hit and false alarm rates on a fixed pair of noise and signal + noise distributions. Then:

- Plot the corresponding ROC point(s) on an ROC graph.
- Explain in words how a liberal versus conservative criterion would manifest in a real detection task (e.g. auditory tone detection).

(3) **Parametric vs. non-parametric analysis.** You have two small groups ($n = 8$ each) of contrast sensitivity measurements that appear non-normally distributed.

- Decide whether to use an independent t-test or a Mann–Whitney U test, justifying your choice based on assumptions.
- If you opt for the Mann–Whitney U, describe how you would report effect size.

(4) **Multiple comparisons in practice.** Suppose you conduct one-way ANOVA on detection thresholds at four different light intensities and obtain a significant main effect. You then perform six pairwise t-tests.

- Calculate the Bonferroni-corrected significance level.
- Explain how the Holm–Bonferroni method would adjust your p- values more efficiently.

3.7 Recommended Reading

- Howell, D. C. (2013). *Statistical Methods for Psychology* (8th ed.). Wadsworth Cengage.
- Field, A., Miles, J., & Field, Z. (2012). *Discovering Statistics Using R* (2nd ed.). Sage.
- Kingdom, F. A. A., & Prins, N. (2016). *Psychophysics: A Practical Introduction* (2nd ed.). Academic Press.
- Macmillan, N. A., & Creelman, C. D. (2005). *Detection Theory: A User's Guide* (2nd ed.). Psychology Press.

CHAPTER

4

Using PsychoPy to Build Experiments

This chapter provides a practical, hands-on guide to implementing psychophysical experiments using the PsychoPy coder environment. We illustrate with two complete examples: a brightness JND (just-noticeable difference) experiment and a serial memory (primacy/recency) task. Each example includes annotated PsychoPy scripts, explanations of key commands, experiment flowcharts (TikZ), and analysis scripts (e.g., Google Colab/Python) to take you from stimulus presentation to data interpretation. No prior coding experience is assumed – comments and textboxes explain concepts as they arise [33].

4.1 Getting Started with PsychoPy

Before writing experiments, ensure PsychoPy is installed on your machine. For local development:

- **Via** pip (recommended for coder mode):

```
# Create and activate a virtual environment
python -m venv PsychoPy_env
source PsychoPy_env/bin/activate # macOS/Linux
PsychoPy_env\Scripts\activate # Windows

# Install PsychoPy
pip install PsychoPy
```

DOI: 10.1201/9788743809456-4

- **Standalone builder:** Download from https://www.PsychoPy.org/ download.html if you prefer a GUI.
- **Note on Google Colab:** PsychoPy cannot present real-time stimuli in Colab. Use Colab for analysis scripts only; run experiments locally.

Running PsychoPy scripts

- Launch the PsychoPy Coder and open your .py script.
- To test incremental changes, use small numbers of trials (e.g., 5–10) before scaling up.
- Use version control (e.g., Git) to track changes in your scripts.

4.2 Example 1: Brightness JND Experiment

In this example, participants judge whether a central dot is darker or brighter than a fixed reference luminance. We use a method of constant stimuli around a reference, record responses, and then fit a psychometric function to estimate the JND. This illustrates basic PsychoPy commands, timing control, response collection, and data logging.

4.2.1 Design and psychophysical rationale

- Task: On each trial, show a central dot (radius 0.1 norm units) whose luminance is $L_{ref} + \Delta L$. Participant presses LEFT arrow if "darker" ($\Delta L \leq 0$) or RIGHT arrow if "brighter" ($\Delta L > 0$).
- **Stimulus set:** A set of 9 equidistant ΔL steps around a reference, e.g. $\Delta L \in \{-0.2, -0.15, \ldots, +0.2\}$.
- **Trials:** Present each ΔL multiple times in random order (e.g., 10 repeats each).
- **Measures:** Hit and false alarm rates for SDT analysis; or proportion "brighter" vs. ΔL to fit psychometric function.

4.2.2 Step-by-step explanation of the brightness JND script

Below we dissect the brightness JND PsychoPy script into functional blocks (Figure 4.1). For each part, we show a minimal code snippet and explain its purpose, key commands, and psychophysical considerations. This approach helps beginners understand how to build experiments modularly.

Imports and setup

Listing 4.1 Importing necessary modules.

```python
from PsychoPy import visual, event, core
import numpy as np
import pandas as pd
import os
```

Figure 4.1 Flowchart of the brightness JND experiment.

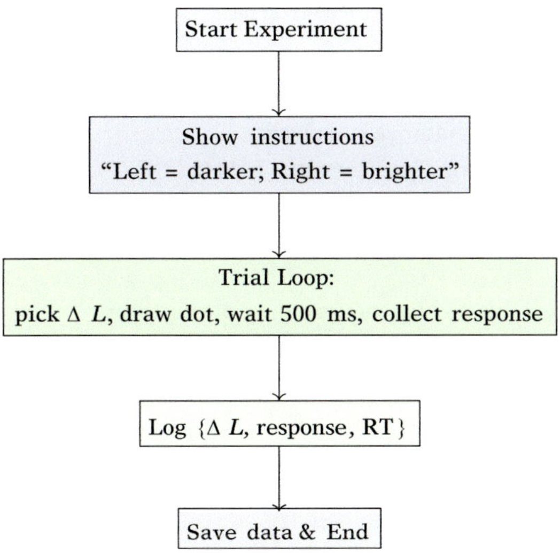

- PsychoPy.visual: for creating windows and stimuli (e.g., shapes, text).
- PsychoPy.event: for handling keyboard/mouse events (collecting responses).
- PsychoPy.core: for timing functions (wait, Clock).
- numpy: numerical operations (e.g., generating luminance steps).
- pandas: convenient data storage and saving to CSV.
- os: for file paths when saving data.

Why these imports?

Psychophysics scripts often mix stimulus presentation (PsychoPy) with data handling (numpy, pandas). Importing only needed modules keeps the namespace clean and startup fast.

Window creation

Listing 4.2 Setting up the display window

```
win = visual.Window(
    size=[800, 600], # window size in pixels
    units='norm',    # normalized coords: (-1,-1) to (1,1)
    fullscr=False, # True for fullscreen mode
    color=[0, 0, 0] # background color (black)
)
win.mouseVisible = False # hide mouse cursor during trials
```

Explanation

- size=[800,600]: window dimensions. In units='norm', these affect actual pixel size but stimuli coordinates use [-1,1].
- units='norm': convenient for centering stimuli (e.g., a circle at pos (0,0)).
- fullscr: fullscreen reduces distractions and ensures stable refresh timing in many setups; for debugging, start with False.
- color=[0,0,0]: RGB triple in [0,1], black here.
- win.mouseVisible=False: hides cursor so it doesn't draw attention or obscure stimuli.

Psychophysical consideration: Screen units

Using units='norm' means all positions and sizes are relative to the window: e.g., radius=0.1 yields a circle at 10

Defining stimulus parameters

Listing 4.3 Generating luminance steps and trial list

```
ref_lum = 0.5 # reference luminance (mid-gray)
n_steps = 9 # number of offset levels
deltas = np.linspace(-0.2, 0.2, n_steps) # deltaL around reference
n_repeats = 10 # repeats per level
# Build a flat list of all trials, then shuffle
trial_list = list(deltas) * n_repeats
np.random.shuffle(trial_list)
```

Explanation

- ref lum = 0.5: baseline luminance (in [0,1]); the dot's brightness is ref lum + ΔL.
- np.linspace(−0.2,0.2,9): generates 9 evenly spaced offsets (e.g., −0.2, −0.15, . . . , +0.2).
- n repeats=10: each offset appears 10 times → total trials = 9 × 10 = 90.
- trial list = list(deltas) * n repeats: creates one list contain- ing each deltaL repeated;
- np.random.shuffle(trial list): randomizes order to avoid order effects.

Alternative: TrialHandler

PsychoPy's data.TrialHandler can manage randomized trials, conditions from CSV, and multiple loops. For simple lists, manual shuffling suffices; for advanced designs (counterbalancing blocks, factorial conditions), consider TrialHandler.

Displaying instructions

Listing 4.4 Instruction screen before trials

```
instr = visual.TextStim(win,
    text="Left = darker, Right = brighter.\nPress any key to start.",
    color=[1, 1, 1], height=0.06
)
instr.draw()
win.flip() # swap buffers: show instruction
event.waitKeys() # wait until participant presses a key
core.wait(0.5) # short pause before first trial
```

Explanation

- visual.TextStim: creates text stimulus. text= can include newline \n.
- height=0.06: relative size in normalized units (approx. 6
- instr.draw(); win.flip(): draw to back buffer and then display.
- event.waitKeys(): blocks until any key press – ensures participant sees instructions before proceeding.
- core.wait(0.5): brief blank interval helps participant prepare; also separates instruction from first trial visually.

Trial loop structure

Before diving into stimulus code, a flowchart of the trial loop is shown in Figure 4.2.

Figure 4.2 Flowchart of a single trial in the brightness JND experiment.

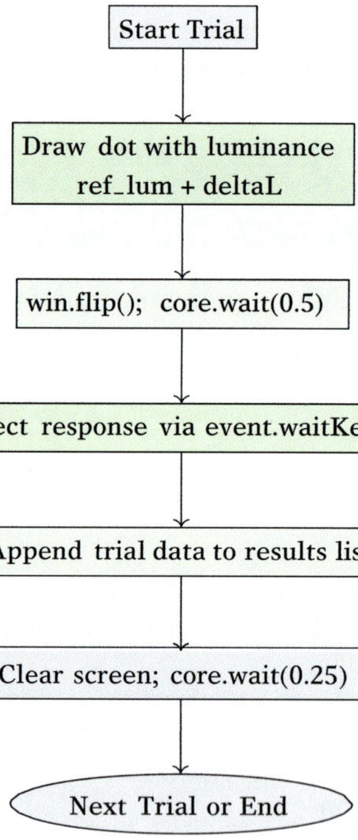

Key points

- Each trial is identical in structure except for the value of ΔL.
- Timing: stimulus shown for 500 ms, then immediate response collection.
- After response, a short inter-trial interval (ITI) of 250 ms.
- Data recorded per trial: ΔL, response ("brighter"/"darker"), reaction time (RT).

Stimulus presentation

Listing 4.5 Drawing and presenting the dot

```
# Inside the trial loop, for each deltaL = d:
lum = np.clip(ref_lum + d, 0, 1) # ensure value stays in [0,1]
dot = visual.Circle(
    win,
    radius=0.1, # size relative to window
    fillColor=[lum, lum, lum],
    lineColor=None,
    pos=(0, 0) # center of screen
)
dot.draw() # draw to back buffer
win.flip() # present the dot
core.wait(0.5) # keep on screen for 500 ms
```

Explanation

- np.clip(...): ensures computed luminance remains valid in [0,1].
- visual.Circle: creates a filled circle. radius=0.1 in normalized units (10
- fillColor=[lum,lum,lum]: grayscale RGB triple; darker or brighter depending on ΔL.
- dot.draw(): writes drawing commands to off-screen buffer.
- win.flip(): swaps buffers, making the dot visible. Precise flip timing is crucial for known stimulus duration.
- core.wait(0.5): holds the frame for 0.5 s. PsychoPy's wait uses a busy-wait loop for millisecond precision.

Response collection and timing

Listing 4.6 Collecting and timing participant response

```
# After showing the dot:
resp_clock = core.Clock() # start timing
keys = event.waitKeys(keyList=['left', 'right', 'escape'])
RT = resp_clock.getTime() * 1000 # reaction time in milliseconds
if 'escape' in keys:
    break # allow experimenter or participant to abort
response = 'brighter' if keys[0] == 'right' else 'darker'
```

Explanation

- core.Clock(): creates a timer; starting it before waitKeys ensures RT measures time from stimulus onset to keypress.
- event.waitKeys(keyList=[...]): waits until one of the specified keys is pressed. Blocks further code until response.
- Multiplying by 1000 converts seconds to milliseconds, a common unit in psychophysics.
- Handling 'escape': graceful exit if participant needs to stop early.
- Mapping keys to semantic responses ("brighter"/"darker") simplifies later analysis.

Data logging

Listing 4.7 Appending data to results list

```
results.append({
    'delta': float(d),
    'response': response,
    'RT':   RT
})
# Clear screen before next trial:
win.flip()
core.wait(0.25) # ITI of 250 ms
```

Explanation

- Use a Python list of dictionaries to accumulate per-trial data. Each dict holds key variables.
- Converting ΔL to float ensures JSON-serializable and consistent CSV format.

- win.flip() with no stimuli drawn clears the screen (shows background) for ITI.
- ITI: short break reduces carryover/adaptation but keeps experiment flow smooth.

Saving data to CSV

Listing 4.8 Saving results to file

```
out_fname = 'jnd_brightness_data.csv'
df = pd.DataFrame(results)
df.to_csv(out_fname, index=False)
print(f"Data saved to {os.path.abspath(out_fname)}")
```

Explanation

- pd.DataFrame(results): converts list-of-dicts into a tabular structure.
- to csv(..., index=False): writes CSV without row indices.
- Using os.path.abspath: helps confirm where file is saved, useful for debugging.

End-of-experiment screen and cleanup

Listing 4.9 Thank-you message and cleanup

```
thanks = visual.TextStim(win, text="Thank you!", color=[1,1,1], height = 0.06)
thanks.draw(); win.flip()
core.wait(1.0) # display for 1 second
win.close() # close window
core.quit() # exit PsychoPy cleanly
```

Explanation

- A brief "thank you" message gives the participant closure.
- win.close() and core.quit() ensure PsychoPy releases resources (window, graphics context).

Notes on enhancements

- **Using TrialHandler:** For more complex designs (e.g., multiple condi- tions in a CSV), replace manual trial list with:

```
from PsychoPy import data
conditions = [{'delta': d} for d in deltas]
trial_handler = data.TrialHandler(conditions, nReps=n_repeats, method='random')
for  trial  in  trial_handler:
    d = trial['delta']
    # ... rest of trial ...
```

This facilitates logging additional metadata and integrates with PsychoPy's data saving.

- **Keyboard vs. Builder settings:** When using the Builder interface, similar code snippets appear in code components; understanding this script helps translate between Builder and Coder modes.
- **Timing verification:** In fullscreen mode, enable win.recordFrameIntervals = True and inspect dropped frames to ensure stimulus durations are accurate.
- **Random seeds:** To reproduce a specific stimulus sequence, call random.seed(123); np.random.seed(123) before shuffling.

Psychophysical and design considerations

Avoiding bias and ensuring validity

(1) **Randomization:** Shuffling trials prevents order effects.

(2) **Balanced repeats:** Ensure each ΔL level appears equal times.

(3) **Catch trials:** Optionally include $\Delta L = 0$ trials to estimate bias separately.

(4) **Instruction clarity:** Clear instructions reduce demand characteristics.

(5) **Session length:** 90 trials × 0.8 s each 1.5–2 minutes of active trials; include breaks if longer.

By understanding each functional block – window setup, stimulus parameterization, instruction display, trial loop structure, stimulus presentation, response collection, data logging, and cleanup – beginners can confidently modify and expand the script (e.g., add practice trials, adaptive staircases, feedback). Breaking the code into these modular parts clarifies the logic and highlights psychophysical best practices.

Explanation of key commands

- visual.Window(...): Creates the display window. Using units='norm' means coordinates range from -1 to 1; central dot at (0, 0).
- win.mouseVisible = False: Hides the cursor so it does not distract.
- np.linspace(-0.2,0.2,9): Defines 9 equally spaced luminance off- sets around the reference.
- np.random.shuffle(trial list): Randomizes trial order to avoid stimulus order effects.
- dot.draw(); win.flip(): draw() writes to back buffer; flip() swaps buffers to present the stimulus.
- core.wait(0.5): Holds the stimulus for 500 ms. Precise timing is critical in Psychophysics.
- event.waitKeys(keyList=[...]): Waits for a keypress; blocks un- til response arrives. Measuring RT via core.Clock().
- win.flip() after response: Clears the screen before the next trial.
- pd.DataFrame(results).to csv(...) : Saves a CSV for later analysis.

Psychophysical considerations

(1) **Timing precision:** PsychoPy's core.wait() uses busy-wait; ensure refresh rate is stable when using fullscreen.
(2) **Randomization:** Fully random trial order avoids predictable patterns.
(3) **Escape key:** Allows aborting experiment safely.
(4) **Number of trials:** Balance precision (more repeats) with participant fatigue.

4.2.3 Data analysis for brightness JND

Since PsychoPy cannot run in Colab, we analyze data in a local Python environment or in Google Colab after uploading JND brightness data.csv.

Loading and descriptive statistics

Listing 4.10 Load data and compute proportions

```
import pandas as pd
import numpy as np
import matplotlib.pyplot as plt
from scipy.optimize import curve_fit
from scipy.stats import norm

```

```
# Load data
df = pd.read_csv('jnd_brightness_data.csv')
# Map responses: 1 = "brighter", 0 = "darker"
df['resp_bin'] = (df.response == 'brighter').astype(int)

# Group by delta and compute proportion "brighter"
grouped = df.groupby('delta').resp_bin.agg(
    count='count',
    prop='mean',
    sd='std'
).reset_index()
print(grouped)
```

Plotting the psychometric function

Listing 4.11 Plot detection probability vs. deltaL

```
plt.errorbar(
    grouped['delta'],
    grouped['prop'],
    yerr=grouped['sd'],
    fmt='o-',
    capsize=5
)
plt.axhline(0.5, color='gray', linestyle='--', label='Chance (50%)')
plt.xlabel('Luminance Offset deltaL')
plt.ylabel('P("Brighter")')
plt.title('Psychometric Data: Brightness JND')
plt.grid(True)
plt.legend()
plt.show()
```

Fitting a cumulative Gaussian

A common choice: cumulative Gaussian (normal CDF [26]). Threshold = ΔL at $P = 0.75$ (2AFC analog) or $P = 0.5$ for yes/no; here we treat yes/no, threshold at $P = 0.5$ for midpoint, but often one uses SDT d' or fitting for $P = 0.75$ in 2AFC. For demonstration, we fit:

$$P(\Delta L) = \Phi\ (\Delta L - \mu)/\sigma$$

where Φ is standard normal CDF, μ is bias, σ relates to slope.

Listing 4.12 Fit cumulative Gaussian to psychometric data

```
# Define cumulative Gaussian
def cum_gauss(x, mu, sigma):
    return norm.cdf((x - mu) / sigma)

# Initial guesses: mu ~ 0, sigma ~ 0.1
popt, pcov = curve_fit(
    cum_gauss,
    grouped[’delta’],
    grouped[’prop’],
    p0=[0, 0.1]
)
mu_hat, sigma_hat = popt
print(f”Fitted mu = {mu_hat:.3f}, sigma = {sigma_hat:.3f}”)

# Plot fit
x_fine = np.linspace(grouped[’delta’].min(), grouped[’delta’].max(), 200)
y_fit = cum_gauss(x_fine, mu_hat, sigma_hat)
plt.plot(x_fine, y_fit, ’-’, label=’Fit’)
plt.scatter(grouped[’delta’], grouped[’prop’], color=’black’)
plt.axvline(mu_hat, color=’red’, linestyle=’--’, label=f”Bias mu={ mu_hat:.3f}”)
plt.xlabel(’deltaL’); plt.ylabel(’P(“Brighter”)’)
plt.title(’Psychometric Function Fit’)
plt.legend()
plt.show()

# Estimate JND: e.g. distance from mu to point where P=0.75:
jnd75 = mu_hat + sigma_hat * norm.ppf(0.75)
print(f”Estimated JND at P=0.75: deltaL ~ {jnd75:.3f}”)
```

Interpreting fit parameters

(1) μ: Point of subjective equality (bias) – if $\mu = 0$, observer tends to respond "brighter" or "darker" even at reference.
(2) σ : Slope inverse – smaller σ means steeper curve (higher sensitivity).
(3) JND (e.g. $P = 0.75$): The intensity difference needed for 75% "brighter" responses (in 2AFC analog).

4.3 Exercise: Building a Serial Memory (Primacy/Recency) Experiment

The goal of this exercise is to guide you, step by step, through creating a serial memory experiment in PsychoPy that probes primacy and recency effects (Figure 4.3). You will incrementally build each component: window setup, stimulus parameterization, sequence presentation, probe phase, response handling, data logging, and analysis. Along the way, consider psychophysical and cognitive principles (randomization, timing control, working memory capacity [24, 55, 42]).

(1) **Define the experimental question and design**
- *Question:* How do set size (number of items in sequence) and judgment type (primacy vs. recency) affect accuracy and reaction time?
- *Design:* Within-subjects design: each participant experiences all set sizes $N \in \{2, 4, 6, 8\}$ and both judgment types.
- *Considerations:* Randomize trial order to avoid practice or fatigue confounds; ensure equal repeats per condition.

Hint: Condition balancing

Decide how many repeats per combination of (set size, judgment). For example, 10 trials each → total trials = 4 set sizes × 2 judgment types × 10 = 80 trials. Later, you may add practice trials or breaks if session is long.

(2) **Window and basic imports**

```
from PsychoPy import visual, event, core
import random, math, pandas as pd, os
```

- Create a PsychoPy window, e.g.:

```
win = visual.Window(size=[800,600], units='pix',
    fullscr=False, color =[0,0,0])
win.mouseVisible = False
```

- *Explanation:* size=[800,600] sets pixel dimensions; units='pix' means all positions/sizes in pixels. Hiding the mouse avoids distraction.

Psychophysical note

Using fixed pixel units is fine for classroom setups. For lab with known monitor distance, consider units='deg' for visual angle control.

(3) **Define stimulus parameters**

- *Color set:* Choose a palette of sufficiently distinguishable colors (e.g., 8 RGB triples).
- *Set sizes:* {2, 4, 6, 8}.
- *Judgment types:* {'primacy', 'recency'}.
- *Trial list:* Build a list of dictionaries, each with fields 'set size' and 'judgement'. Example code:

```
colors = [
[1,0,0], [0,1,0], [0,0,1], [1,1,0],
[1,0,1], [0,1,1], [0.5,0.5,0.5], [1,0.5,0]
]
set_sizes = [2,4,6,8]
trials = []
for N in set_sizes:
for _ in range(10): # 10 repeats per condition
trials.append({'set_size': N, 'judgement ': 'primacy'})
trials.append({'set_size': N, 'judgement ': 'recency'})
random.shuffle(trials)
```

- *Explanation:* Sampling 10 primacy and 10 recency for each *N* yields balanced conditions. Shuffling avoids predictable sequences.

(4) **Instruction screen**

```
instr = visual.TextStim(win,
text="You will see a sequence of colored squares.\ nAfterwards,
    decide which appeared FIRST or LAST.\nPress any key to
    begin.",
color=[1,1,1], height=24
)
instr.draw(); win.flip()
event.waitKeys(); core.wait(0.5)
```

- *Tip:* Keep instructions concise; mention key mapping (e.g., LEFT arrow for left square, RIGHT arrow for right square).
- Add a brief practice block (e.g., 4 trials) before the main experiment so participants understand the sequence task.

(5) **Trial loop: sequence presentation**

- For each trial dictionary in trials:
  - Extract *N* = trial['set size'] and judgement.
  - *Choose colors:* trial colors = random.sample(colors, N) ensures distinct items.
  - *Compute positions:*
    - Place items on an imaginary circle (radius in pixels, say 150 px).
    - Compute equidistant angles with a random rotation offset:

```
rotation_offset = random. uniform(0, 360)
positions = []
for i in range(N):
angle = math.radians(rotation_offset + i *(360.0/N))
x = 150 * math.cos(angle)
y = 150 * math.sin(angle)
positions.append((x,y))
random.shuffle(positions)
```

- *Fixation:* Show a "+" at center for 500 ms:

```
fix = visual.TextStim(win, text='+', color=[1,1,1],
    height=40)
fix.draw(); win.flip(); core .wait(0.5)
```

- *Present sequence:* Loop through zip(trial colors, positions):

```
for color_val, pos in zip( trial_colors, positions) :
sq = visual.Rect(win, width =50, height=50,
fillColor=color_val, lineColor=color_val, pos =pos)
sq.draw(); win.flip(); core. wait(0.8) # display 800 ms
win.flip(); core.wait(0.2) # ISI 200 ms
```

Timing consideration

Consistent display (800 ms) and ISI (200 ms) allow encoding without overlap. If too fast, participants may miss items; too slow increases memory load. Pilot to choose durations.

(6) **Probe phase: selecting and displaying two items**

- *Select two indices:*

```
indices = random.sample(range(N), 2)
early_idx, late_idx = min(indices), max(indices)
```

- *Random left/right assignment:*

```
if random.choice([True, False]):
left_idx, right_idx = indices[0], indices[1]
else:
left_idx, right_idx = indices[1], indices[0]
```

- *Determine correct side:*

```
if trial['judgement']=='primacy':
correct = 'left' if left_idx==early_idx else 'right'
prompt = "Which appeared FIRST? Left or Right?"
else: # recency
correct = 'left' if left_idx==late_idx else 'right'
prompt = "Which appeared LAST? Left or Right?"
```

- *Draw probe stimuli:*

```
left_sq = visual.Rect(win, width=50, height=50,
fillColor=trial_colors[left_idx],
lineColor=trial_colors[left_idx],
pos=(-150,0))
right_sq= visual.Rect(win, width=50, height=50,
fillColor=trial_colors[right_idx],
lineColor=trial_colors[right_idx],
pos=(150,0))
qstim = visual.TextStim(win, text=prompt,
pos=(0,-200), color=[1,1,1], height=24)
left_sq.draw(); right_sq.draw(); qstim.draw()
win.flip()
```

- *Explanation:*
  - Positions (–150, 0) and (150, 0) place probes left and right.
  - Prompt tells participant which judgment to make.
  - Randomizing side prevents spatial biases.

(7) **Response collection and logging**

```
clk = core.Clock()
keys = event.waitKeys(keyList=['left','right', 'escape'])
RT = clk.getTime() * 1000 # in ms
if 'escape' in keys:
break  # allow early exit
resp = keys[0]
accuracy = 1  if  resp==correct else 0
# Log data, e.g.:
```

```
    results.append({
        'set_size': N,
        'judgement': trial['judgement'],
        'accuracy': accuracy,
        'RT': RT,
        'probe_left_serial': left_idx+1,
        'probe_right_serial': right_idx+1
    })
    # Inter-Trial Interval
    win.flip(); core.wait(0.5)
```

Data considerations

Include both serial positions (left idx+1, right idx+1) so you can later analyze serial position effects. Recording RT in ms allows comparing speed across conditions.

(8) **Saving data at end of experiment**

```
out_fname = 'serial_memory_data.csv'
df = pd.DataFrame(results)
df.to_csv(out_fname, index=False)
print(f"Data saved to {os.path.abspath(out_fname)}")
```

- *Tip:* If the experiment may be aborted mid-session, consider saving partial data periodically (e.g., every block).

(9) **Analysis outline.** After running the experiment and saving serial memory data.csv, analyze:

- *Accuracy vs. set size and judgment:* Group by ['set size','judgement'] to compute mean accuracy; plot curves to observe capacity limits and primacy/recency differences.
- *RT vs. set size and judgment:* Similarly, examine how response times change.
- *Serial position effects:* Use recorded probe serial positions to plot accuracy as a function of actual serial position (e.g., positions 1. . . N) separately for primacy and recency conditions [56].
- *Statistical tests:* Use repeated-measures ANOVA or mixed-effects models to test effects of set size and judgment type.

Figure 4.3 Flowchart for one trial of the serial memory experiment.

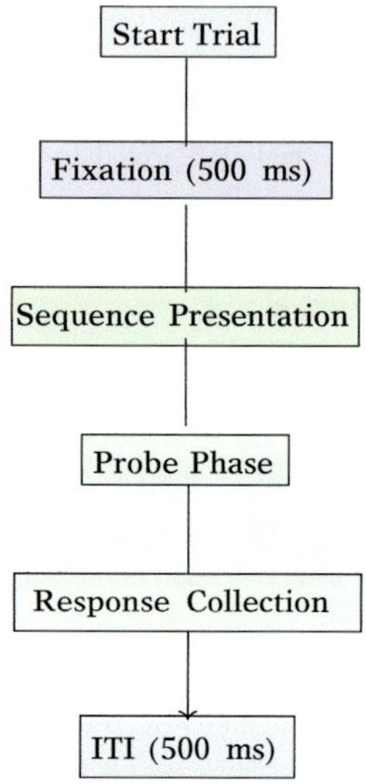

Example analysis snippet

```
import pandas as pd
import matplotlib.pyplot as plt

df = pd.read_csv(’serial_memory_data. csv’)
# Mean accuracy
summary = df.groupby([’set_size’,’ judgement’]).accuracy.mean().
        reset_index()
# Plot:
for  j  in [’primacy’,’recency’]:
data = summary[summary.judgement==j]
plt.plot(data[’set_size’],        data[’accuracy’], marker=’o’, label=j.
        capitalize())
plt.xlabel(’Set Size’); plt.ylabel(’Mean Accuracy’)
plt.legend(); plt.grid(True); plt.show ()
```

(10) **Extensions and variations**

- *Vary timing*: change presentation duration or ISI to examine encoding time effects.
- *Increase set sizes beyond 8*: test capacity limits further.
- *Introduce distractors*: present an irrelevant stimulus during ISI to probe interference.
- *Adaptive difficulty*: adjust N based on participant performance to find maximal working memory span.

Research consideration

Always pilot new variations to ensure timing and difficulty are appropriate; monitor for fatigue if session length increases.

Explanation of key commands

- random.sample(colors, N): Chooses *N* distinct colors for the sequence.
- Position computation: Equidistant angles around a circle with radius 150 pixels; random rotation ensures unpredictability.
- Timing: 800 ms presentation, 200 ms ISI – consistent encoding.
- Probe selection: Randomly pick two sequence indices, assign left/right to avoid spatial bias.
- Response mapping: LEFT/RIGHT arrow; measure RT via core.Clock().
- Data logging: Record set size, judgement type, accuracy, RT, and serial positions for later analysis.

4.3.1 Serial position profiles

Optionally, examine how accuracy depends on the actual serial position of the probed item:

Listing 4.13 Serial position effects

```
# Add a column indicating which serial position was correct for primacy /recency
# For example, for primacy: correct serial position = 1; for recency: = set_size
# But since probe positions vary, one can group by probe_serial (left/ right), judgment,
    and correctness
# Extract actual probed position and correctness
```

```
# Already stored in 'probe_pos_left' and 'probe_pos_right' but need to derive actual target position
# Example for primacy:
df['target_pos'] = df.apply(lambda row: 1 if row.judgement=='primacy' else row.set_size, axis=1)
# Now, for each serial position p, compute accuracy when that position was probed
# But requires knowing which probe corresponded to target;
# Better: re-record during experiment which serial position is target side, then group by that
```

4.4 Best Practices, Debugging, and Reproducibility

Version control

Keep your PsychoPy scripts in a Git repository. Commit before and after major changes. Document experiment parameters (e.g., number of trials, durations) in comments or a separate README.

Debugging tips

(1) **Test with few trials:** Use small loops (e.g. 5 trials) to ensure logic and timing are correct.
(2) **Print statements/logging:** Temporarily print trial variables to console for verification.
(3) **Escape mechanism:** Ensure pressing ESC cleanly quits and saves partial data if needed.
(4) **Monitor timing:** In fullscreen, check for dropped frames; use win.recordFrameIntervals for advanced debugging.-

Reproducibility

(1) **Seed random generators if you need reproducible stimuli sequences:** random.seed(123); np.random.seed(123).
(2) **Document environment:** Python/PsychoPy versions, OS, screen resolution.
(3) **Save raw data:** Keep CSVs and backup; include metadata (timestamp, participant ID).

4.5 Running Experiments Remotely or in the Lab

- For classroom demonstrations, project the PsychoPy window on a large screen and have students respond via keyboard.
- For online or remote data collection, consider PsychoJS (PsychoPy's online counterpart) or adapt scripts accordingly.
- Always pilot on the target hardware to verify timing, colors, and audio (if used).

4.6 Conclusion

This chapter guided you through building two fully functional psychophysical experiments in PsychoPy: a brightness JND task and a serial memory task. You have seen how to structure scripts, control timing, randomize stimuli, collect and save data, and analyze results in Python. By following these examples and adapting them to your own research questions, you can move seamlessly from theory to practice, embodying the irreverent yet rigorous spirit of modern psychophysics. Happy experimenting!

Answer Keys

Chapter 1

Q1. Reconstructing Weber's Experiment

1. **Modern replication setup:**
   - Use a precise digital force sensor or electronic weight scale as your reference (e.g. 500 g).
   - Present comparison weights in ascending and descending series (e.g. ±5 g steps).
   - Ask the participant to indicate "heavier" or "lighter" relative to the reference.
   - Record the smallest weight difference at which judgment flips – this is the JND.

2. **Potential confounds and controls:**
   - *Temperature drift:* Metal weights change slightly in size/weight – calibrate sensors before each session and maintain room at 22 °C.
   - *Participant posture/fatigue:* Muscle tension can bias force readings – standardize arm posture, give rest breaks, alternate ascending/descending runs.
   - *Auditory cues:* Handling weights can make noise – use silent handling or headphones with masking noise.

Q2. Fechner's Logarithmic Law in Context

1. **Philosophical and experimental rationale:**
   - Fechner built on Weber's finding that $\Delta I/I$ is constant, integrating $dS = k\, dI/I$ yields $S = k \ln I + C$.

- A logarithm compresses large stimulus ranges into a smaller perceptual scale – mirroring how sensations "feel" less sensitive at high intensities.

2. **Modern examples:**
   - *Loudness:* Decibels are defined as 10 log10(I/I_0).
   - *Brightness:* Human perception of luminance follows a log–log power law in many contexts.
   - In audio playback, doubling physical intensity (watts) does not double perceived loudness – consistent with a logarithmic mapping.

Q3. Stevens' Power Law and its Critique

1. **Comparison with Fechner's law:**
   - Fechner: $S \propto \ln I$ (logarithmic).
   - Stevens: $S \propto I^n$ (power function), where exponent n varies by modality (e.g. $n \approx 0.33$ for brightness, $n \approx 0.67$ for loudness).
   - When data deviate systematically from a straight line on a semi-log plot, a power-law fit often yields smaller residuals.

2. **Thought experiment:**
   - *Brightness matching:* Present a reference brightness and allow participants to adjust a second patch until it "looks twice as bright."
   - If participants choose $I_{match} \approx k\, I_{ref}^{1/3}$, this suggests $n = 1/3$.
   - Fit a power function to the collected pairs (I_{ref}, I_{match}) via regression on log–log axes to estimate n.

Q4. Evaluating Classical Paradigms

1. **Method of limits**
   - *Strength:* Simple to administer; converges quickly on threshold by bracketing.
   - *Limitation:* Anticipation and habituation biases; less precise around true threshold due to discrete steps.
   - *Modernization:* Adaptive staircases (e.g. QUEST) automatically adjust step size based on responses, reducing total trials and bias.

2. **Method of constant stimuli**
   - *Strength:* Unbiased sampling across stimulus range; yields full psychometric curve.

- *Limitation:* Very time-consuming; many near-threshold trials wasted above/below threshold.
- *Modernization:* Use Bayesian adaptive methods (e.g. ZEST) to concentrate trials near threshold, improving efficiency.

3. **Method of adjustment**
   - *Strength:* Fast and intuitive; participant controls stimulus directly.
   - *Limitation:* High variability across observers; depends on participant strategy and step sizes.
   - *Modernization:* Implement as a slider in PsychoPy with fine-grained increments; log intermediate settings to model bias and variability.

Q5. Historical Reflection

1. **Quantitative measurement's influence:**
   - Psychophysics introduced rigorous experimental control and statistical analysis into psychology, paving the way for Wundt's laboratories and modern cognitive science.
   - Emphasis on replication and threshold estimation shifted psychology from introspective anecdotes to reproducible data.

2. **"Irreverent psychology" and debate:**
   - Early critiques of introspection (e.g. Titchener vs. behaviorists) forced methods that rely on external behavior rather than internal reports.
   - The "method of stimulus error" debate (whether participants should name the physical stimulus rather than sensation) led to the clarity of forced-choice paradigms in psychophysics.

Chapter 2

Q1. ITD and ILD Cues

1. **Maximum ITD calculation:**
   Head diameter d = 0.18 m, speed of sound c = 343 m/s. Maximum interaural path length ≈ diameter:

$$\Delta t_{max} = \frac{d}{c} = \frac{0.18}{343} \approx 0.000525s = 525\mu s.$$

2. **Cue interaction at 30°:**
   - *ITD:* At (30°), path difference ≈ $d \sin 30° = 0.18 \times 0.5 = 0.09$ m ⇒ $\Delta t \approx 0.09/343 \approx 262$ μs.
   - *ILD:* Broadband sound will be slightly louder in the right ear due to head shadow, especially at frequencies >1.5 kHz.
   - *Integration:* The auditory system combines ITD cues (dominant at low frequencies <1.5 kHz) with ILD cues (dominant at higher frequencies) via neural populations in the medial and lateral superior olives, yielding a fused percept of a source at 30° right.

Q2. Weber–Fechner vs. Stevens' Power Law

1. **Functions with $k = 1$:**

$$S_{\text{Fechner}}(I) = \ln I, \qquad S_{\text{Stevens}}(I) = I^{0.33}.$$

For I from 1 to 100:

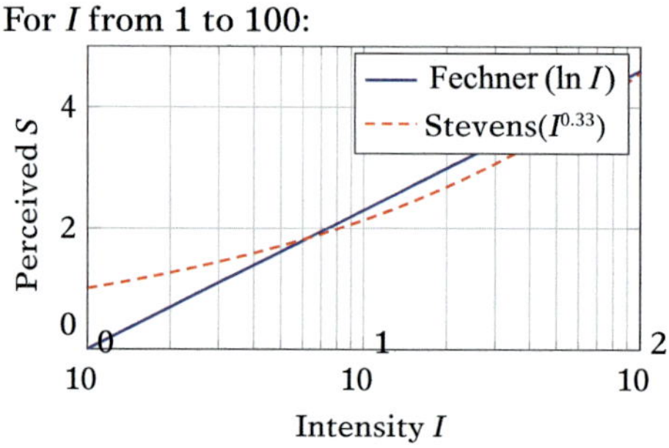

2. **Dim stimulus behavior:**
   - As $I \to 1^+$, $\ln I \to 0$ but with infinite slope at $I = 1$; very dim intensities yield large relative changes in ln I.
   - Stevens' power law rises more gradually from $S(1) = 1$, with finite slope.
   - *Conclusion:* For very dim stimuli near detection threshold, Stevens' law often fits empirical data better (shallower initial slope), whereas Fechner's law exaggerated sensitivity changes at low intensities.

Q3. Two-point Discrimination

1. **Apparatus:** Calibrated digital calipers with blunt tips; two probes can be set at separations from 1 mm to 10 mm.

2. **Separation levels:** e.g. {1, 2, 3, 4, 5, 6, 8, 10} mm.

3. **Method:**
   - Use *method of constant stimuli*: present single- vs. dual-probe stimuli in random order; participant reports "one point" or "two points."
   - Each separation level presented ≥10 times; single-probe catch trials interleaved to estimate guess rate.

4. **Threshold estimation:** Fit a psychometric curve (e.g. logistic) to proportion "two points" vs. separation; threshold = separation at 75% correct.

5. **Bias control:**
   - Include catch trials (0 mm separation) to measure false-alarm rate.
   - Use signal detection theory to compute *d* at each separation, separating sensitivity from response bias.

Q4. Olfactory Adaptation

1. **Protocol:**
   - *Baseline:* Measure detection threshold for citrus odor (e.g. via method of limits).
   - *Adaptation phase:* Expose participant to a fixed concentration for 2 minutes.
   - *Post-adaptation tests:* At intervals (0, 2, 5, 10 minutes), present a mid-level concentration and ask for intensity rating on a scale (e.g. 0–100).

2. **Quantifying decay:**
   - Plot intensity rating vs. time; fit an exponential decay $R(t) = R_0\, e^{-t/\tau}$.
   - Time constant τ indexes adaptation speed.

3. **Accounting for individual differences:**
   - Normalize each participant's ratings by their baseline R_0.
   - Use mixed-effects modeling to include random intercepts for participant.

Chapter 3

Q1. Design Your Own Psychometric Task

1. **Example answer: Visual contrast detection**
   - **Independent variable:** Michelson contrast of a sine-wave grating, range C = [0.01, 0.02, 0.04, 0.08, 0.16, 0.32].

- **Dependent measure:** Yes/no detection – participant presses "space" if they see the grating, "none" if not.
- **Psychometric function:** Weibull

$$P(C) = 1 - (1 - \gamma)\ \exp -(C/\alpha)^{\beta}$$

  because it accommodates a guess rate γ and can model shallow or steep slopes via β .
- **Threshold and slope estimation:** Fit the Weibull by maximum-likelihood to the proportion detected at each C.
  - Threshold α is the contrast yielding $P = 1 - (1 - \gamma)e^{-1} \approx 63\%$ detection.
  - Slope β controls the steepness around threshold.

Q2. Criterion Shifts in SDT

1. **Effect on hit/false alarm rates:** With a noise distribution $N(\mu_N = 0, \sigma = 1)$ and a signal + noise distribution $N(\mu_S = 2, \sigma = 1)$, moving the decision criterion c to the left increases both hit rate (H) and false alarm rate (F); moving c to the right decreases both.

2. **ROC plot with precomputed points:** We choose four criterion values $c \in \{-1, 0, 1, 2\}$. For each:

$$F = \Phi\ (c - 0)/1\ , \qquad H = \Phi\ (c - 2)/1\ ,$$

   where Φ is the standard normal CDF. Numerically:

$$\{(F, H)\} \approx \{(0.1587, 0.0013), (0.5, 0.0228), (0.8413, 0.1587), (0.9772, 0.5)\}.$$

3. **Liberal vs. conservative criterion:**
   - A *liberal criterion* (low c) yields high hit rates but also high false alarms – useful when misses are costly.
   - A *conservative criterion* (high c) yields low false alarms but also lower hit rates – useful when false alarms are costly.

Q3. Parametric vs. Non-parametric Analysis

1. **Choice of test:** Data appear non-normally distributed and sample size is small ($n = 8$ per group) $\Longrightarrow$ Mann–Whitney U test is preferred over independent t-test, since it does not assume normality.

2. **Effect size for Mann–Whitney U:** Compute the standardized rank-sum difference, for example:

$$r = \sqrt{\frac{Z}{N}} \quad N = n_1 + n_2$$

where Z is the normal-approximation of the U-test statistic. Report r alongside U and p.

Q4. Multiple Comparisons in Practice

1. **Bonferroni correction:** With $\alpha = 0.05$ and six pairwise tests, the per-test significance level is

$$\alpha_{Bonf} = \frac{0.05}{6} \approx 0.0083.$$

2. **Holm–Bonferroni adjustment:**
   - Order the six p-values from smallest to largest: $p_{(1)} \leq p_{(2)} \leq \cdots \leq p_{(6)}$.
   - Compare $p_{(1)}$ to $\alpha/6$, $p_{(2)}$ to $\alpha/5, \ldots, p_{(6)}$ to $\alpha/1$.
   - Reject hypotheses sequentially until the first non-significant comparison; all subsequent tests are considered non-significant.

   This method is uniformly more powerful than the simple Bonferroni.

Bibliography

[1] Eugenio Bertelli et al. *Anatomy of the eye and human visual system*. Piccin Nuova Libraria spa, 2019.

[2] Rafal Bogacz, Eric Brown, Jeff Moehlis, Philip Holmes, and Jonathan D Cohen. The physics of optimal decision making: a formal analysis of models of performance in two-alternative forced-choice tasks. *Psychological review*, 113(4):700, 2006.

[3] Edwin Garrigues Boring. *A history of experimental psychology*. Century Company, 1929.

[4] Thomas Brandt, Marianne Dieterich, and Doreen Huppert. Human senses and sensors from aristotle to the present. *Frontiers in Neurology*, 15:1404720, 2024.

[5] Susana TL Chung and Gordon E Legge. Comparing the shape of contrast sensitivity functions for normal and low vision. *Investigative ophthalmology & visual science*, 57(1):198–207, 2016.

[6] Hugh Coolican. *Research methods and statistics in psychology*. Psychology press, 2017.

[7] Dennis Dacey, Orin S Packer, Lisa Diller, David Brainard, Beth Peterson, and Barry Lee. Center surround receptive field structure of cone bipolar cells in primate retina. *Vision research*, 40(14):1801–1811, 2000.

[8] Walter H Ehrenstein and Addie Ehrenstein. Psychophysical methods. In *Modern techniques in neuroscience research*, pages 1211–1241. Springer, 1999.

[9] Mark D Fairchild. *Color appearance models*. John Wiley & Sons, 2013.

[10] Robert L Fantz. Visual experience in infants: Decreased attention to familiar patterns relative to novel ones. *Science*, 146(3644):668–670, 1964.

[11] Gustav Theodor Fechner. *Elemente der Psychophysik, Vol. 1 & 2*. Breitkopf & Ha¨rtel, 1860. Founding text of psychophysics – includes Method of Limits, Fechner's law.

[12] Gustav Theodor Fechner. *Elements of Psychophysics (translated by H. E. Adler)*. Holt, Rinehart & Winston, 1966. English translation of Fechner's seminal work.

[13] J. Feldman. Information-theoretic signal detection theory. *Psychological Review*, 128(5):976–987, 2021. Contemporary extension of SDT principles.

[14] Allan Ferguson. Quantitative estimates of sensory events. *Nature*, 130(3291):810–810, 1932.

[15] Karl R Gegenfurtner and Daniel C Kiper. Color vision. *Annual review of neuroscience*, 26(1):181–206, 2003.

[16] Melvyn A Goodale and A David Milner. Two visual pathways–where have they taken us and where will they lead in future? *Cortex*, 98:283–292, 2018.

[17] D. M. Green and J. A. Swets. *Signal Detection Theory and Psychophysics*. John Wiley & Sons, 1966. Seminal text introducing SDT to psychology.

[18] Michael J Hautus, Neil A Macmillan, and C Douglas Creelman. *Detection theory: A user's guide*. Routledge, 2021.

[19] Michael Heidelberger. *Nature from Within: Gustav Theodor Fechner and His Psychophysical Worldview*. University of Pittsburgh Press, 2004. Biography and philosophical context of Fechner's work.

[20] Ira J Hirsh and Charles S Watson. Auditory psychophysics and perception. *Annual review of psychology*, 47(1):461–484, 1996.

[21] Laurent Itti and Christof Koch. Computational modelling of visual attention. *Nature reviews neuroscience*, 2(3):194–203, 2001.

[22] K. O. Johnson and S. S. Hsiao. Neural coding and the basic law of psychophysics. *The Neuroscientist*, 8:111–121, 2002. Bridges psychophysics with neural mechanisms.

[23] Masakazu Konishi. Coding of auditory space. *Annual review of neuroscience*, 26(1):31– 55, 2003.

[24] Steven J Luck and Edward K Vogel. The capacity of visual working memory for features and conjunctions. *Nature*, 390(6657):279–281, 1997.

[25] Neil A Macmillan. Signal detection theory. *Stevens' handbook of experimental psychology: Methodology in experimental psychology*, 3:43–90, 2002.

[26] Keith A May and Joshua A Solomon. Four theorems on the psychometric function. *PLoS One*, 8(10):e74815, 2013.

[27] D. McNicol. *A Primer of Signal Detection Theory*. Allen & Unwin, 1972. Accessible introduction to SDT concepts.

[28] Sebastian Merchel and M Ercan Altinsoy. Psychophysical comparison of the auditory and tactile perception: A survey. *Journal on Multimodal User Interfaces*, 14(3):271–283, 2020.

[29] M-Marsel Mesulam. From sensation to cognition. *Brain: a journal of neurology*, 121(6):1013–1052, 1998.

[30] John C Middlebrooks. Sound localization. *Handbook of clinical neurology*, 129:99–116, 2015.

[31] Lone Nikolajsen and Kristian Friesgaard Christensen. Phantom limb pain. *Nerves and Nerve Injuries*, pages 23–34, 2015.

[32] Haluk Ogmen, Bruno G Breitmeyer, and Reginald Melvin. The what and where in visual masking. *Vision research*, 43(12):1337–1350, 2003.

[33] Jonathan W Peirce. Psychopy – psychophysics software in python. *Journal of neuroscience methods*, 162(1-2):8–13, 2007.

[34] Denis G Pelli and Bart Farell. Psychophysical methods. *Handbook of optics*, 1:29–1, 1995.

[35] W. W. Peterson, T. G. Birdsall, and W. C. Fox. The theory of signal detectability. *Transactions of the IRE Professional Group on Information Theory*, 4(4):171–212, 1954. One of the earliest formal accounts of signal detection theory applied to radar and perception.

[36] Marco Piccolino and Nicholas J Wade. Galileo galilei's vision of the senses. *Trends in neurosciences*, 31(11):585–590, 2008.

[37] Howard Rachlin. What mu¨ller's law of specific nerve energies says about the mind. *Behavior and Philosophy*, pages 41–54, 2005.

[38] Josef P Rauschecker. Auditory and visual cortex of primates: a comparison of two sensory systems. *European Journal of Neuroscience*, 41(5):579–585, 2015.

[39] Carolyn Rovee-Collier, Kristin Hartshorn, and Manda DiRubbo. Long-term maintenance of infant memory. *Developmental Psychobiology: The Journal of the International Society for Developmental Psychobiology*, 35(2):91–102, 1999.

[40] Melissa Saenz and Dave RM Langers. Tonotopic mapping of human auditory cortex. *Hearing research*, 307:42–52, 2014.

[41] Nelli H Salminen, Patrick JC May, Paavo Alku, and Hannu Tiitinen. A population rate code of auditory space in the human cortex. *PLoS One*, 4(10):e7600, 2009.

[42] Rakesh Sengupta. Modeling visual working memory using recurrent on-center off-surround neural network with distance dependent inhibition. *Scientific Reports*, 15(1):23000, 2025.

[43] Rakesh Sengupta, S Bapiraju, and David Melcher. Big and small numbers: Empirical support for a single, flexible mechanism for numerosity perception. *Attention, Perception, & Psychophysics*, 79(1):253–266, 2017.

[44] Rakesh Sengupta, Bapi Raju Surampudi, and David Melcher. A visual sense of number emerges from the dynamics of a recurrent on-center off-surround neural network. *Brain research*, 1582:114–124, 2014.

[45] Nicholas Shea. Distinguishing top-down from bottom-up effects. *Perception and its modalities*, pages 73–91, 2015.

[46] Michael T Shipley, Matthew Ennis, and Adam C Puche. The olfactory system. In *Neuroscience in medicine*, pages 611–622. Springer, 2008.

[47] S. S. Stevens. The direct estimation of sensory magnitudes – loudness. *American Journal of Psychology*, 69:1–25, 1956. Early presentation of Stevens' power law.

[48] S. S. Stevens. On the psychophysical law. *Psychological Review*, 64:153–181, 1957. Core formulation of Stevens' power function.

[49] John A Swets. *Signal detection theory and ROC analysis in psychology and diagnostics: Collected papers*. Psychology Press, 2014.

[50] Hans J Ten Donkelaar, Jonas Broman, and Peter van Domburg. The somatosensory system. In *Clinical neuroanatomy: brain circuitry and its disorders*, pages 171–255. Springer, 2020.

[51] Kaisa Tiippana. What is the mcgurk effect? *Frontiers in psychology*, 5:725, 2014.

[52] Bernhard Treutwein. Adaptive psychophysical procedures. *Vision research*, 35(17):2503–2522, 1995.

[53] Bijal P Trivedi. Gustatory system: The finer points of taste. *Nature*, 486(7403):S2–S3, 2012.

[54] Bhavesh K Verma and Rakesh Sengupta. Emergence of behavioral phenomena and adaptation effects in human numerosity decoder using recurrent neural networks. *Scientific Reports*, 13(1):19571, 2023.

[55] Lakshmi Sree Vindhya, R Gnana Prasanna, Rakesh Sengupta, and Anuj Shukla. Modeling primacy, recency, and cued recall in serial memory task using on-center off-surround recurrent neural network. In *International Conference on Machine Learning, Optimization, and Data Science*, pages 405–414. Springer, 2024.

[56] Nancy C Waugh and Donald A Norman. Primary memory. *Psychological review*, 72(2):89, 1965.

[57] Ernst H. Weber. *De pulsu, resorptione, auditu et tactu: Annotationes anatomicae et physiologicae*. Ko¨hler, 1834. Weber's original work introducing the concept of just noticeable differences.

[58] Felix A Wichmann and N Jeremy Hill. The psychometric function: I. fitting, sampling, and goodness of fit. *Perception & psychophysics*, 63(8):1293–1313, 2001.

[59] John T Wixted. The forgotten history of signal detection theory. *Journal of experimental psychology: learning, memory, and cognition*, 46(2):201, 2020.

[60] Wilhelm Wundt. Ueber das weber'sche gesetz. *Philosophische Studien*, 2:1–36, 1885. Wundt's analysis of Weber's law within physiological psychology.

Index

For Product Safety Concerns and Information please contact our
EU representative GPSR@taylorandfrancis.com Taylor & Francis
Verlag GmbH, Kaufingerstraße 24, 80331 München, Germany